Between Criminalization and Protection

Transnational Crime

Volumes published in this Brill Research Perspective are listed at *brill.com/rptc*

Between Criminalization and Protection

The Italian Way of Dealing with Migrant Smuggling and Trafficking within the European and International Context

By

Vincenzo Militello and Alessandro Spena

BRILL

LEIDEN | BOSTON

This paperback book edition is simultaneously published as issue 2.1–2 (2018) of *Transnational Crime*, DOI:10.1163/24680931-12340007.

Typeface for the Latin, Greek, and Cyrillic scripts: "Brill". See and download: brill.com/brill-typeface.

ISBN 978-90-04-40166-2 (paperback)
ISBN 978-90-04-40172-3 (e-book)

This book is printed on acid-free paper and produced in a sustainable manner.

Contents

Between Criminalization and Protection
The Italian Way of Dealing with Migrant Smuggling and Trafficking within the European and International Context 1
Vincenzo Militello and Alessandro Spena
Abstract 1
Keywords 1
Introduction 1
Abbreviations 4
Part 1. Migrant Smuggling: a Normative and Phenomenological View from Italy 5
Alessandro Spena
1.1 Preliminary Terminological Remarks 5
1.2 A Very Brief Historical Introduction to the Criminalization of Migrant Smuggling in Italy 7
1.3 Archetypes of Migrant Smuggling 8
1.4 Cross-border vs. Inland Smuggling 9
1.4.1 *Inbound Smuggling: the Prototypical Form* 10
1.4.2 *Some Phenomenological Features of Inbound Smuggling toward Italy* 11
1.4.2.1 An In-depth Excursus on Inbound Smuggling by Sea 13
1.4.3 *Outbound Smuggling and Solidarity between States* 17
1.4.4 *Some Phenomenological Features of Outbound Smuggling from Italy* 20
1.4.5 *Inland Smuggling: Is Transnationality a Necessary Characteristic of the Crimes of Smuggling?* 21
1.4.6 *Why Is Inland Smuggling Considered a Less Serious Crime than Cross-border Smuggling?* 23
1.5 The Structure of Conduct 24
1.5.1 *Inbound Smuggling as a Typically Collective Crime?* 24
1.5.2 *Crimes of Cross-border Smuggling as Inchoate Crimes: from Spatial to Aspirational Borders* 25
1.5.3 *Inland Smuggling as a Resultative Crime* 28
1.5.4 *Rescuers and Mediated Smugglers: the Scope of Italian Criminal Jurisdiction* 29

1.6 Profit and No-profit Smuggling 33
1.6.1 *Rescue and Humanitarian Smuggling* 35
1.6.2 *NGOs as Humanitarian Smugglers? the Luventa Case* 38
1.7 Basic and Aggravated Forms of Smuggling 41
1.8 Why Punish Migrant Smuggling? 42
1.8.1 *The EU Approach: Smuggling as Complicity in Irregular Migration* 44
1.8.1.1 The Rights of the Smuggled Persons in EU Law 45
1.8.1.2 The EU Action Plan against Migrant Smuggling (2015–2020) 46
1.8.2 *The UN Approach: Smuggling as Exploitation* 47
1.8.3 *What Is/Are the Good/s Protected by Italian Law on Smuggling?* 48
Bibliography 52
Part 2. Trafficking in Human Beings vs. Migrant Smuggling: a Dangerous Relationship 55
Vincenzo Militello
2.1 The Double Track of Human Trafficking: an Introduction 55
2.2 The Different Approaches toward Countering Trafficking: Human Rights vs. Security and the Need for Integration 58
2.3 A New Integrated Perspective on International Counter-action 62
2.4 Prevention as a Criminal Policy Tendency inside the UN Protocol 64
2.5 The Victims' Stance and the Difference between Trafficking and Smuggling 65
2.6 The Consequences of the Distinction in European Legal Texts 67
2.7 The Consequences of the Distinction within the Italian Legal System 69
2.8 The Consequences for Internal Case Law: Multiplicity of Offences or (Apparent) Conflict of Norms? 75
2.9 Short Conclusion 78
Bibliography 78

Between Criminalization and Protection

The Italian Way of Dealing with Migrant Smuggling and Trafficking within the European and International Context

Vincenzo Militello and Alessandro Spena
Department of Law, University of Palermo
vincenzo.militello@unipa.it; alessandro.spena@unipa.it

Abstract

This double issue is focused on migrant smuggling and human trafficking. Both subjects are mainly treated from an Italian perspective; however, since these crimes have a generally transnational character, the analysis also takes international (UN) and supranational (EU) measures into account. Moreover, in both parts, the legal perspective is supplemented by the phenomenological/criminological one (based on both media reports and judicial case-studies), so as to grasp the practical aspects emerging from the different ways in which migrant smuggling and human trafficking are *de facto* committed: in particular, the links between these two and other crimes are underscored, as well as the involvement of criminal organizations in their perpetration. Finally, both parts are driven by a human rights-oriented approach, which gives relevance to dignity of persons as a fundamental meta-value of our legal systems.

Keywords

migrant smuggling – human trafficking – Italian law – EU facilitation package – EU Directive 2011/36/EU – Protocols to the UN Convention against transnational organized crime

Introduction

This double issue is devoted to the dark side of human mobility, that is migrant smuggling and, linked with it, human trafficking. Both subjects will be mainly treated from an Italian perspective; however, due to their generally transnational character, the analysis will necessarily require that international and

 | DOI:10.1163/9789004401723_002

supranational actions/measures also be taken into account. Moreover, in both parts, the legal perspective will be supplemented by the phenomenological/criminological one, through which we try to provide our work with a realistic dimension aimed at grasping the practical aspects of our subjects emerging from the different ways in which such crimes as migrant smuggling and human trafficking are *de facto* committed.

The first part of this double issue, in particular, will be specifically concerned with migrant smuggling in/toward Italy. On a normative level, this will basically entail an interpretation of the relevant Italian legislation; in doing this, however, attention will be focused on the most crucial questions, while bypassing the many minutiae that could be evoked by a too detailed analysis: since this double issue is principally addressed to an international readership, it will be more useful to provide a general conceptual account of the Italian approach to migrant smuggling than with a disorienting labyrinth of secondary problems. At the same time, and for the same reasons, the analysis of Italian legislation will be ideally located within the relevant international (UN and EU) context, in order to evaluate whether and to what extent the former conforms to tendencies and obligations coming from the latter.

Moreover, this normative reconstruction will be given "criminological solidity" by locating it against the background of an analysis of the most relevant phenomenological aspects of smuggling in/toward Italy. Since the aim of this criminological investigation is that of infusing the analysis of criminal norms with sufficient concreteness, it will not be placed in a different section: it will rather be intertwined with interpretation of legal norms, in the hope that this will result in a clearer definition of the overall picture. In practice, a—hopefully wide, though not exhaustive—geo-phenomenological map will be provided, concerning the events of smuggling in/toward Italy and based on a taxonomy of their main routes and executive modalities. The material to do this will essentially be drawn from judicial investigations and decisions, obtained either directly or indirectly (i.e., through media reports). This material being non-exhaustive, the phenomenological reconstruction provided here does not claim to have statistic value nor to be able to represent reality in all its shades. It rather aspires to having an illustrative value, so as to give a cross-section, both significant and reliable, of the actual shape of the phenomenon considered. Moreover, since this double issue was delivered in March 2018, it does not take into consideration phenomenological developments that have taken place, in Italy, since then. This, however, does not impinge on the conceptual framework that is here provided for.

Lastly, the first part of this double issue will also be concerned with one of the thorniest questions regarding smuggling: how is the role of the smuggled foreigner evaluated by law? Is he or she seen as a victim or as a co-author of the crime? The difficulty of this question derives from the tremendous ambiguity characterizing smuggling in this respect. While the adjacent case of human trafficking is univocally interpreted as having the trafficked subject as the victim of the crime, the same cannot be said of smuggling. A reason for this lies in the fact that smuggling represents the point of discharge of two conflicting energies, namely, on the one hand, the concern (the obsession?) of states with controlling and regulating foreigners' entrance and stay in their territory and, on the other hand, the extremely difficult conditions in which the journey of smuggled foreigners generally takes place, fraught with dangers and constantly exposed to the risk of being mistreated and exploited. This is the crucial point: smuggling is, of course, a way by which foreigners try to bypass the state's control over its borders; however, it entails—almost structurally—an exploitation of foreigners themselves and very scarce attention to their primary needs and dignity. The smuggled subject enters the picture both as the agent who makes use of smuggling in order to reach his or her goals and as the smugglers' instrument, as the object of their exploiting activity, and as the means of which smugglers make use in order to reach their goals in their turn.

The second part of this double issue tackles, instead, human trafficking, from a multilevel perspective. First of all, it takes into account the human rights-oriented approach to the matter, which gives relevance to dignity of persons as a meta-value of the legal system. Second, it also takes into account the importance of a law enforcement action aimed, in particular, at fighting the phenomenon in virtue of its links with other new forms of criminality. In the face of their diversity, the necessity will be underlined of integrating both these approaches, coherently with the holistic way of fighting human trafficking that has taken hold at a supranational level.

In this perspective, it will be underscored that the UN Protocol against Trafficking in Persons not only sets forth traditional repressive penal measures, but also urges a more comprehensive approach, also based on prevention, cooperation between states and protection and assistance for the victims. Around this latter aspect, according to the received [current] interpretation, there revolves the difference from migrant smuggling, which is the object of a different protocol to the UN convention on transnational organized crime.

The rigid separation between these two crimes is also reaffirmed in the EU legal instruments. Italian law, in its turn, relies on it: conduct of trafficking is based on the final exploitation of migrants and is aimed at protecting their individual personalities (art. 601 c.p.), while migrant smuggling is taken into account as a form of facilitation of irregular immigration and is regulated *extra codicem* in art. 12 TUIMM.

However, the border between these two phenomena is frequently blurred, as various kinds of relationships can exist between them. Italian judges, however, have frequently applied this distinction too strictly, whereas the osmotic character of the links between these two criminal conducts should be given due relevance in order to obtain a more adequate protection of human dignity.

Abbreviations

c.p.	*codice penale* (Italian penal code)
Cass.	*Corte di Cassazione* (Italian Court of Cassation)
d.l.	*decreto-legge* (law-decree)
d.lgs.	*decreto legislativo* (legislative decree)
ECHR	European Convention on Human Rights
ECtHR	European Court of Human Rights
FD	Facilitation Directive
FFD	Facilitation Framework Decision
g.i.p.	*Giudice per le indagini preliminari* (Judge of preliminary investigations)
ICCPR	International covenant on civil and political rights (New York, 1966)
l.	*legge* (statute law)
Sec.	Section (subdivision of *Corte di Cassazione*)
Trib.	*Tribunale* (Tribunal)
TUIMM	*Testo unico delle disposizioni concernenti la disciplina dell'immigrazione e norme sulla condizione dello straniero* (Italian consolidated act concerning immigration)
UNODC	United Nations Office on Drugs and Crime
UNPS	United Nations Protocol against Smuggling

Part 1. Migrant Smuggling: a Normative and Phenomenological View from Italy

Alessandro Spena

1.1 Preliminary Terminological Remarks

Let me begin with some preliminary terminological remarks.

This first part of the double issue will be focused on such types of conduct as procuring the irregular entrance of foreigners in the territory of a state, procuring their irregular exit therefrom, and favouring their irregular stay therein. Taken together, these three typologies of conduct are frequently referred to, within the Italian juridical debate, as facilitation of irregular immigration; however, it should be clear that they do not necessarily entail "immigration" in the strict sense: the term "immigration" refers, indeed, to the fact of durably settling within a territory different from that of origin,[1] while neither (irregular) entrance in a state territory, nor—and even less—(irregular) exit therefrom necessarily entail such durable settlement.

At an international level (mostly—but not only—in English-speaking countries), in both daily and technical legal language, it is more common to refer to these same types of conduct as "smuggling of migrants" or "migrant smuggling." Exactly because of their being so widely used, in this paper I will mainly stick to these expressions. However, it must be clarified from the outset that they also have their shortcomings. The verb "to smuggle" basically means "to take things or people to or from a place secretly and often illegally."[2] It corresponds to the German verb "schmuggeln" (both deriving from low German "smukkeln" or "smuggelen")[3] and to the Italian "contrabbandare" ("to smuggle" is indeed synonym for "to contraband"). So-called migrant smuggling departs from this original semantic core from both a normative and a phenomenological perspective. From both these perspectives, for instance, migrant smuggling has to do not only with "introducing" foreigners into a given territory or "taking

1 For instance, the *Cambridge Dictionary* defines "immigration" as "the act of someone coming to live in a different country" (https://dictionary.cambridge.org/dictionary/english/immigration). Even more clearly, the *Oxford English Dictionary* defines it as "The action of coming to live permanently in a foreign country" (https://en.oxforddictionaries.com/definition/immigration).

2 https://dictionary.cambridge.org/dictionary/english/smuggle.

3 See, e.g., https://en.oxforddictionaries.com/definition/smuggle.

out" foreigners from one, but also, as I have said earlier, with helping them to irregularly sojourn therein, which does not presuppose that they have irregularly entered (think of foreigners who have regularly entered and are helped to overstay their tourist visa or residence permit).

From a different perspective, it should be underlined that smuggling and contraband are both linked to the idea of trading: the smuggling/contraband of x means that x is being illegally traded on a black market. This does not apply, however, when migrants are involved (at most, it may apply to human trafficking, on which see Part Two), not at least in the sense that smuggled migrants are being traded: they are rather the smugglers' clients. The expression "smuggling *of migrants*" (appearing, for instance, in the UNPS) is therefore incorrect, and should be avoided in favour of "*migrant* smuggling", in which the word "migrant" indicates not the object of commerce, but the background against which the smugglers' conduct places itself.

Moreover, neither on a normative level nor on a phenomenological one does migrant smuggling require secrecy or concealment, which instead is distinctive of the general notion of smuggling (as also of the analogous notion of contraband):[4] the adjective "irregular" in such syntagmas as "irregular entrance", "irregular transit", and "irregular stay" is not a synonym of "secret", "hidden" or "concealed." Criminal norms against migrant smuggling do not (usually) require that the foreigner be helped to enter *secretly* the territory of a state, or to remain *hidden* therein. And, if we look beyond norms, we can see that many cases of migrant smuggling take place openly, in full daylight (think of those particularly eye-catching cases of migrant smuggling, in which multitudes of foreigners, squeezed in unseaworthy boats, reach Southern European shores in the middle of the day).

What in the general concept of "smuggling" is expressed by the element of "concealment", in the specific concept of "migrant smuggling" should thus be seen as completely absorbed, more properly, by the element of "irregularity", that is by the "illegality", or "unlawfulness", of entrance into or stay in the state's territory, or of exit therefrom. It is with these reservations in mind that I will be using the expression hereafter.

4 See, e.g., the definition of "contraband" in the *Cambridge Dictionary* as "goods that are brought into or taken out of the country secretly and illegally" (https://dictionary.cambridge.org/dictionary/english/contraband).

1.2 A Very Brief Historical Introduction to the Criminalization of Migrant Smuggling in Italy

Italy began to criminalize migrant smuggling long before this became an inter- and supranational obligation. The first Italian criminal norm expressly concerned with this phenomenon was art. 3, sub-sec. 6, d.l. 416/1989,[5] punishing "whoever carries out activities aimed at favouring the entrance of foreigners into the territory of the state in violation of the norms of this decree."[6]

A similar type of offence was included in all those legislative measures that, during the 1990s, relentlessly tried to amend d.l. 416/1989: l. 39/1990 (which converted d.l. 416/1989 into law), but also the stream of so-called *Dini decrees*[7] enacted and reiterated between the end of 1995 and the end of 1996. It can also be found in l. 40/1998 (art. 10), which finally succeeded in substituting d.l. 416/1989, as well as in art. 12 d.lgs. 286/1998 (*Testo unico delle disposizioni concernenti la disciplina dell'immigrazione e norme sulla condizione dello straniero* [henceforth: TUIMM]),[8] which, in its turn, substitutes art. 10, l. 40/1998, and still represents the fundamental norm criminalizing migrant smuggling in Italy.

In the meanwhile, starting with the new millennium, the phenomenon of human smuggling became the subject of an increasingly detailed and pervasive inter- and supranational legal regulation. For our purposes, it will suffice to mention the principal sources of this regulation, which are the Protocol against the Smuggling of Migrants by Land, Sea and Air, supplementing the United Nations Convention against Transnational Organized Crime (henceforth: UNPS),[9] and the EU package against smuggling, made up of the so-called

---

5 D.l. 416/1989, in its turn, was the first legislative measure through which Italy attempted to provide itself with a systematic regulation of immigration. Before then, the regulation of the matter could be found in: *a*) some articles of both the Consolidated act on public security (TULPS), enacted in 1931, and its implementing regulation, enacted in 1942, all of which, according to their location, took immigration into account only from a securitarian perspective; *b*) l. 943/1986, specifically concerning the work of non-EU immigrants; *c*) some occasional, though frequent (four between '87 and '88), measures specifically aimed at regularizing the position of non-EU workers.

6 A prodrome of this crime could be found in art 12, l. 943/1986, which, however, was specifically concerned with foreign workers, and not with foreigners in general.

7 Named after Lamberto Dini, who was the Italian premier in 1995 and then the Italian minister of foreign affairs in 1996.

8 Which means "Consolidated act of norms concerning immigration and the legal status of foreigners." The TUIMM aims at gathering and coordinating, in a single normative document, the most relevant Italian norms on immigration.

9 It was adopted by General Assembly Resolution 55/25 and entered into force on 28 January 2004.

Facilitation Directive (henceforth: FD)[10] and the so-called Facilitation Framework Decision (henceforth: FFD).[11] The contents of these two sources (UN and EU) are only partly overlapping, as they are informed, to a good extent, by divergent logics. In what follows, I will not present these contents and logics autonomously, but in parallel with the analysis of Italian legislation, so as to understand the extent to which this latter conforms to international trends, as well as the extent to which it instead departs from them.

1.3 Archetypes of Migrant Smuggling

Over the years, art. 12 TUIMM has undergone many reformulations, only partly due to the need to implement international requirements; for the most part these reformulations have been manifestations of the strong anxieties that, cyclically, come back to haunt the Italian political debate when the so-called "fight against illegal immigration" is concerned (which generally happens in periods of electioneering).

Evidence of this anxiety-laden approach—as well as of the uncertainties and confusion it engenders—is the intricacy and prolixity of the existing shape of art. 12. It is made up of 25 sub-sections, the majority of which are the result of interpolations following the original enactment of the TUIMM in 1998, as is graphically shown by the stream of sub-sections bis, ter, quarter etc. that can be found in it. As frequently happens, such a high number of normative contents, which is a sign of continual changes of mind, makes the regulation not only quantitatively overabundant, but also qualitatively poor, vague and inconsistent. Conducts (particularly in sub-secs. 1 and 3: see infra, § 1.5) are described in a redundant and confused way; the language used is, at times, inaccurate (as is the case with the definition of outbound smuggling in secs. 1 and 3: see infra, § 1.4.3); the meaning of some expressions is far from clear (which can be said, for instance, of the expressions referring to the aim of profit requirement in sub-secs. 5 and 5 bis: see infra, § 1.6).

In what follows, I will try to simplify this convoluted set of norms, by reconstructing the general models that can be discerned beyond the details. In this spirit, we can say that, in the existing version of art. 12 TUIMM, different

10 Council Directive 2002/90/EC of 28 November 2002 defining the facilitation of unauthorised entry, transit and residence.

11 Council Framework Decision 2002/946/JHA of 28 November 2002 on the strengthening of the penal framework to prevent the facilitation of unauthorised entry, transit and residence.

possible archetypes of migrant smuggling can be seen, corresponding to different ways in which Italian law criminalizes this phenomenon. Three are, in particular, the fundamental categories of migrant smuggling as a crime: inbound smuggling (procuring the irregular entrance of foreigners into the territory of a state), outbound smuggling (procuring their irregular exit therefrom), and inland or internal smuggling (favouring their irregular stay therein). These three crimes, in their turn, can be placed in other categories, depending on the features they have in common. From this perspective, the basic dichotomy is between cross-border smuggling (in which inbound and outbound smuggling are brought together) and, again, inland smuggling, which depends on whether smuggling entails cross-border transportation of the foreigner. Other relevant dichotomies are between profit smuggling (forms of smuggling only punishable if committed for profit) and no-profit smuggling (forms of smuggling punishable even if not committed for profit); inchoate smuggling (forms of smuggling defined in the inchoate mode) and resultative smuggling (forms of smuggling in which conduct is only punishable if effectively *resulting in* facilitating irregular foreigners). Finally, beside the basic forms of migrant smuggling, other forms can be distinguished in which conduct is surrounded by aggravating circumstances.

In what follows, I will reconstruct these different models of smuggling. In particular, in the spirit of simplification to which I have previously committed myself: a) I will only take into consideration those sub-sections of art. 12 (1, 2, 3, 3 ter, 5 and 5 bis) from which those models can be extracted, leaving aside the many others which limit themselves to regulating specific aspects of the matter; b) I will analyse these same sub-sections only to identify their grounding principles, passing over the many points of detail which are irrelevant to the definition of reference models; c) for each of these models, I will try to reconstruct—if possible and appropriate—their wider legal-philosophical and politico-philosophical implications.

1.4 Cross-border vs. Inland Smuggling

The various forms of smuggling can be grouped, first of all, according to whether the smuggler's conduct necessarily entails the smuggled foreigner to be moved, and in particular his or her crossing (either from outside to inside or from inside to outside) a state border. In fact, even though the idea of migrant smuggling is generally associated with transportation of people, the phenomenon in its legal and social dimension can also be independent from this element: beside forms of smuggling structurally having a kinetic and transnational character (cross-border smuggling), others instead have an endogenous and intra-border character, consisting in favouring not foreigners' irregular crossing of a border, but their irregular stay within a state territory in which they already find themselves (inland smuggling).

1.4.1 *Inbound Smuggling: the Prototypical Form*

From a vectorial point of view (that is, according to the *direction* of the foreigner's border-crossing, taken from the perspective of the state criminalizing his or her being smuggled), the category of cross-border smuggling can be further divided into inbound and outbound smuggling.

By inbound smuggling I mean the smuggling of a foreigner from outside of a territory to its inside. Italian law criminalizes this conduct in art. 12, sub-secs. 1 and 3 (to which sub-secs. 3 bis and 3 ter also refer), describing it, in both sub-sections, as the action of "whoever, in violation of this consolidated act, promotes, leads, organizes, finances or carries out *the transportation of foreigners into the territory of the state*, or performs other acts directed to procure the [foreigner's] *illegal entrance in the territory of the state*." Arts. 4, sub-sec. 3, 22, sub-sec. 5 bis, letter a and 27 quater, sub-sec. 10, letter a, refer to this crime as "facilitation of clandestine immigration toward Italy"; we already know, however, that this is an incorrect terminology (see above, § 1.1).

Inbound smuggling is the paradigmatic form of migrant smuggling. Not without reason it is the first form in which the phenomenon was criminalized in Italian law (starting from art. 3, sub-sec. 6, d.l. 416/1989); just as it is no coincidence that it is the first form of smuggling dealt with by art. 12.

Above all, the centrality of inbound smuggling is consistent with the fundamental values and aims for which states criminalize smuggling: values and aims principally revolving (as will be shown throughout this part) around such ideas as territorial sovereignty and state borders' intangibility (or better still, the idea of their selective openness, with states claiming to have the right to choose who to admit within their territory).[12]

Further evidence of this centrality can also be derived from international law sources, which in fact treat inbound smuggling as the fundamental form of the phenomenon. For instance, art. 3 UNPS defines the very concept of "Smuggling of migrants" precisely as "the procurement, in order to obtain, directly or indirectly, a financial or other material benefit, of the illegal *entry* of a person into a State Party of which the person is not a national or a permanent resident" (where "Illegal entry" means "*crossing borders* without complying with the necessary requirements for legal entry into the receiving State"). On

12 See, e.g., Cass., Sec. I, 17.1.2017, no. 7416.

the other hand, inbound smuggling represents the first hypothesis taken into account by the FD, with art. 1, sub-sec. 1, letter a, requiring "Each Member State [to] adopt appropriate sanctions on […] any person who intentionally assists a person who is not a national of a Member State to *enter* […] the territory of a Member State in breach of the laws of the State concerned on the *entry* […] of aliens."

1.4.2 *Some Phenomenological Features of Inbound Smuggling toward Italy*

From a phenomenological point of view, different forms of inbound smuggling toward Italy can be distinguished. According to the route they follow, we can distinguish, first of all, between inbound smuggling by sea (coming from the south) and overland inbound smuggling (coming from the north). The former takes place, in particular, along three different pathways: from Greece (but also, in very few cases, directly from Turkey)[13] to Puglia or Calabria (south-eastern route);[14] from Tunisia to the western Sicilian shores (south-western route); from Egypt or Libya to South Italy (central Mediterranean route). Inbound overland smuggling, instead, mostly comes from Slovenia; less often from France; even more seldom from Austria.[15]

Different routes entail different criminological characteristics. Whether, in order to commit the crime, a sea must be crossed or instead just a line of land heavily affects the shape of action. First, it determines what vehicles must be used: smuggling by sea necessarily entails using some kind of boat or vessel; by contrast, overland smuggling is generally committed by concealing foreigners in cars' or vans' secret compartments, or, even more simply, by taking them—either by car or on foot—across the border, trying to bypass police checks.

Moreover, while foreigners by sea are generally smuggled in large quantities (particularly along the central Mediterranean route), overland smuggling always concerns small groups of foreigners. This is certainly due to the different

13 Generally, however, inflows from Turkey (mostly originating in such countries as Afghanistan and Pakistan, as well as Bangladesh and Sri Lanka) pass through Greece, from which they then divide between the Balkan route, the sea route towards the South of Italy and the route towards North Africa (Libya, Egypt, but also Tunisia and Algeria). For a sociological reconstruction of smuggling routes toward Southern Europe, see Anna Triandafillidou, *Migrant Smuggling. Irregular Migration from Asia and Africa to Europe* (Palgrave MacMillan 2012). See also Europol, 'Migrant Smuggling in the EU', Feb. 2016 (available at: https://www.europol.europa.eu/publications-documents/migrant-smuggling-in-eu).

14 See, for instance, Cass., Sec. I, 2.3.2017, no. 32408 (concerning the transportation of twenty Syrians from southern Peloponnese to Locri, in Calabria).

15 See, e.g., Cass., Sec. I, 11.12.2017, no. 1525.

vehicles to be used and to their different capacity; but probably it is also due to the fact that the organization and execution of smuggling by sea are more complex and demanding activities than those required by overland smuggling; it is thus understandable that smugglers by sea try to maximize their profit and to minimize their costs by gathering as many passengers as possible in every single "shipment."

Moreover, as we will see later on (§ 1.4.2.1.1), the fact of there being a sea between the state of departure and that of arrival gives smugglers the possibility of performing their conduct in particularly complex ways (with migrants abandoned in the high seas waiting for rescuers to take over), which could not be easily replicated in cases of overland smuggling.

The different complexity of the required activities—including the different availability of vehicles, as well as the necessity to deal with corrupt public officials—also affects both the costs of the service and the smugglers' profit margin, both of which are obviously higher in cases of smuggling by sea.[16] This, in turn, heavily contributes to determining the characteristics of the subjects involved as smugglers. We will see later on (§ 1.4.2.1.1) that smuggling along central Mediterranean routes is characterized by being mainly in the hands of transnational criminal organizations, whereas inbound overland smuggling, as emerges in judicial investigations or news reports, is basically performed either by individuals or by small and poorly organized groups.

Moreover, smuggling by sea (most of all, along central Mediterranean routes) is generally committed in manifest ways, since the Egyptian and Libyan smugglers frequently play on the Italian, European and international system of sea rescue in order to accomplish their goal. Overland smuggling, instead, normally happens secretly. While, in other words, migrants arriving by sea frequently try to enter the Italian territory *by surrendering themselves to* (and thus, *by acting through*) *the authorities*, by whom they are rescued and from whom they receive first aid (even though, after disembarking, they may try to escape), those arriving by land try instead *to evade authorities* and to bypass their checks. This may have its main reason, once again, in the different characteristics of the routes: crossing the Mediterranean sea in unseaworthy boats or dinghies is a much more eye-catching and difficult enterprise than crossing an imaginary line traced on the land: in this last case, unlike the former, it is rarely necessary to rely on the authorities' assistance.

Finally, the social and political features of the state of departure can also influence the executive modalities of smuggling. Smuggling by sea frequently comes from states (in the present time, this is especially true of Libya) marked

16 See, e.g., Cass., Sec. I, 11.12.2017, no. 1525.

by huge political instability, if not by the absence of a centralized and effective political power; this creates an overall situation in which criminal groups and organizations can be kings, which, for instance, gives them the possibility to confine up to thousands of migrants as well as to subject them to inhuman treatment and torture. For obvious reasons, this could hardly happen when the smuggling route originates in such European countries as Slovenia, Austria or France.

Notwithstanding all the said differences, smuggling by sea and overland smuggling have something in common: they both happen in evidently irregular ways; neither foreigners disembarking in Sicily after being rescued from shipwreck nor those caught crouching in vans will claim to be entering regularly, in compliance with the state regulation on foreigners' entrance. Under this perspective, they are in opposition to another way of committing the crime, which can be dubbed *fraudulent smuggling*: in cases of fraudulent smuggling, foreigner's irregular entrance is arranged through document counterfeiting making it appear regular.[17] Interestingly, in this way of committing the crime, both foreigners and Italians are normally involved as co-authors: this is due to the fact that fraudulent smuggling requires, on the one hand, that certain subjects (themselves foreigners) act as intermediaries with would-be migrants, contacting them directly in their countries of origin, and, on the other hand, that other subjects (who need to be either Italian citizens or at least regular residents) fictitiously declare to be ready to hire would-be migrants, or to enter into a relationship with them on the existence of which they can rely in order to apply for regularization.

1.4.2.1 An In-depth Excursus on Inbound Smuggling by Sea

Even though all the abovementioned forms of inbound smuggling deserve in-depth consideration, I will limit myself here to dealing at length with only one of them, that is, inbound smuggling by sea: not because it is particularly eye-catching and over-represented in the media, but rather because, as I will try to show, some of its manifestations are particularly interesting from both a conceptual and a criminological perspective.

To begin with, it should be noticed that the expression "smuggling by sea" is inextricably committed to the—necessarily one-sided—perspective of the state criminalizing it: a perspective understandably limited to giving relevance to such events only to the extent that they intercept the state's criminal

17 See, e.g., Cass., Sec. I, 22.5.2014, no. 28819 (stipulation of a false lease agreement aimed at favouring the issuing of visas); Cass., Sec. I, 15.4.2016, no. 48402; Cass., Sec. V, 17.10.2017, no. 51615; Cass., Sec. I, 23.11.2017, no. 57440.

jurisdiction and sovereignty. Seen instead from the migrant's perspective, that expression only catches one portion of the whole situation. On the one hand, indeed, if we set aside Tunisians or Moroccans directly arriving at the Italian shores, crossing the Mediterranean sea never represents the first segment of the migrants' journey, nor their first contact with smugglers. According to what they declare, the great majority of foreigners that disembark on the Italian shores arrive from countries that are located far away from North Africa: in 2017,[18] 61% of foreigners irregularly arriving in Italy by sea declared they were from Nigeria (15%), Ivory Coast (8%), Guinea (8%), Bangladesh (8%), Mali (6%), Eritrea (6%), Sudan (5%) and Senegal (5%); a percentage that could further increase if account was taken of the remaining 29% of "other nationalities", the vast majority of which will probably be non-Mediterranean ones.

But the expression "smuggling by sea" is also one-sided in the opposite sense, which has to do with the role that Italy plays in the migratory projects of those foreigners who irregularly arrive on the Italian shores: many of these projects only consider our country as an intermediate step, not as their final destination (which generally is represented, instead, by North European countries such as Germany, France, the UK, and Scandinavian countries). Crossing the Mediterranean again appears to be only a portion of the whole migratory project.

Having said this, in what follows I will limit myself to underscoring some characteristics, which I find particularly relevant from a criminological viewpoint, emerging from recent events of inbound smuggling by sea. Relying on judicial case-studies, I will underline, in particular, significant differences between smuggling along central Mediterranean routes and smuggling from the south-eastern route (specifically, from Tunisia).

1.4.2.1.1 *Central Mediterranean Route*

Smuggling from Egypt and—most of all—from Libya is, among other things, characterized by peculiar executive modalities (which I will call "smuggling interruptus") and by the massive presence of criminal organizations. Importantly, as will become clearer during the exposition, both these characteristics heavily impinge on the smuggled migrants' interests.

18 Data of the Ministry of the Interior, 31 December 2017 (http://www.libertaciviliimmigrazione.dlci.interno.gov.it/sites/default/files/allegati/cruscotto_statistico_giornaliero_31-12-2017.pdf).

Smuggling interruptus. First of all, smuggling activities coming from both Egypt[19] or Libya[20] are frequently performed in complicated ways through which smugglers try to avoid being caught, and their vessels being seized and destroyed, by the Italian authorities: in particular, migrants are initially embarked on a sufficiently capacious and solid vessel (so-called mother-ship), followed by one or more other boats or dinghies (son ships), which instead are substantially unseaworthy. Having arrived in the high seas, migrants are forced to get off the mother-ship and to continue their journey on the son ships; piloting these ships are some of the smuggled migrants themselves (who completely lack the necessary expertise), provided with a satellite phone to use in order to call for help when the mother-ship has gone, leaving the migrants at the mercy of the sea. Very rarely will the ship succeed in autonomously reaching the Italian territorial sea; most frequently they will be rescued by private vessels (fishermen, NGOs) finding themselves in the vicinity, or by the vessels of the state responsible for the corresponding SAR (search and rescue) area. Rescued migrants are brought to the nearest "place of safety" (which is frequently in Italy).

Criminal organizations. Another feature of smuggling along the central Mediterranean route is the significant involvement of criminal organizations.[21] There is huge evidence, for instance, of the existence of smugglers' criminal organizations operating in Libya (but also in Egypt), with a generally clear distribution of roles and tasks among participants; these organization have a transnational character—they therefore fully fall under the UNPS—both because they have connections with sending and transit states (such as Niger) and because their action is aimed at producing effects in other states (at least, in the states of destination). Moreover, participating in these organizations are people from different nationalities: for instance, according to a recent judicial investigation in Palermo, a Libyan criminal organization operating in Sabratha is composed of a Libyan boss, other Libyan citizens in charge of arranging the departures, one or more Malians acting either as fixers or as cashiers, and approximately twenty Sub-Saharans (mostly Nigerians) acting as gaolers.

The need to resort to gaolers comes from the fact that migrants are not mere "clients" of these smugglers: from judicial investigations it has also emerged, indeed, that migrants arriving in Libya with a view to going on toward Europe

---

19 See, e.g., Trib. Catania, Sec. V, 17.12.2015.

20 See, e.g., Cass., Sec. I, 28.2.2014, no. 14510; Cass., Sec. I, 30.1.2017, no. 14694 (a case in which the *scafista* piloted the boat out to the high seas, then turned the engine off and tried to make himself out to be a passenger among the others).

21 See, e.g., Cass., Sec. I, 28.2.2014, no. 14510; Trib. Catania, Sec. V, 17.12.2015; Procura della Repubblica di Palermo, Decreto di fermo, no. 7001, 7.5.2017.

are frequently kidnapped by criminal groups and then put in prison camps.[22] Witnesses speak of one of these camps (the so-called *Fatal camp*) in which approximately one thousand would-be migrants were held. Life in smugglers' camps can be extremely hard, with gaolers creating a climate of terror: violence, tortures, rapes, even killings have been widely reported. Migrants remain confined therein until a ransom is paid, either by their relatives at home or by themselves, through their forced labour.

Voluntary migrants? Interestingly, the sense of this payment is double: on the one hand, it counts as the ransom for their release, but, on the other hand, it also counts as the price for their journey forward; it can be said that these migrants are kept hostage until they pay for their ticket to Europe. This makes it particularly difficult to define these situations according to current conceptual categories: though these migrants are frequently referred to as "economic migrants" (in order to specify that they are not "forced" migrants, escaping war or persecution in their homelands and thus entitled to apply for asylum, but are instead persons who voluntarily leave in search of better living conditions), their position, when they arrive in Italy after having transited through Libya, is far more complicated than the expression "economic migrants" indicates; many of them admittedly leave behind them difficult but not completely unlivable situations; in general, it can be said that they voluntarily leave their home country and that they are voluntarily trying to reach Europe. The events they undergo during their journey, however, end up making the original voluntariness of their choice hardly relevant and insufficient to qualify them fully as "voluntary" or "economic" migrants when they arrive in Italy: when these persons finally succeed in embarking toward our shores (frequently, as we have seen, only to be abandoned in the high seas), they have been subjected to so many deprivations and torments that it is perfectly meaningful to say that they are escaping tortures and persecution.

Obviously, the same considerations also affect the legal qualification of the criminal's conduct: if, as is generally argued,[23] the main criterion to distinguish between smuggling and trafficking is the consent of the migrant, this distinction becomes extremely difficult to maintain in the cases considered here; it is not by chance that Italian judges, in many cases, interpret those two crimes as

---

22 See, e.g., Cass., Sec. I, 30.1.2017, no. 14694; Procura della Repubblica di Palermo (n 21).

23 See, e.g., Jacqueline Bhabha and Monette Zard 'Smuggled or Trafficked?' [2006] Forced Migration Review 6 (underlining how the UN Protocols are framed around the dichotomy between coercion [trafficking] and consent [smuggling], but also pointing out that "the majority of migration strategies and circumstances defy easy categorisation"); Matilde Ventrella, *The Control of People Smuggling and Trafficking in the EU: Experiences from the UK and Italy* (Routledge 2016) 139.

mutually compatible, punishing the same subjects for the same conduct both as smugglers and as traffickers (see infra, Part Two).

1.4.2.1.2 *South-western Route*

Smuggling along the route from Tunisia to western Sicily, at least in some cases, has quite different characteristics than those just seen. Recent judicial investigations have brought to light, indeed, a more "elitist" form of the crime, characterized, first of all, by very different travelling conditions:[24] the ships used are decidedly safer and more rapid (small fishing boats or hydrofoils), the duration of the trip is shorter (also because of the fact that Tunisia and Sicily are relatively near) and only small groups of foreigners are loaded in. As a consequence, the price of the journey is higher and the typologies of "passengers" using this channel is understandably different ("relatively wealthy North-Africans [...] who can bear the cost of this exclusive transit")[25] from those embarking from Libya.

Given the shortness of the crossing, there is neither need nor space to resort, in such cases, to the *smuggling interruptus* stratagem: along the South-western route, smuggling generally takes place in secret, with ships trying to go unnoticed by the Italian and European authorities.

What these cases of smuggling have in common with the previous ones is, however, that they are mainly handled by transnational criminal organizations, involving different persons in charge of different roles (bosses, brokers, skippers, crew).

1.4.3 *Outbound Smuggling and Solidarity between States*

Inbound smuggling is opposed to outbound smuggling, that is, the smuggling of foreigners outside of state borders. It must be clarified from the onset that outbound smuggling can be seen as different from inbound smuggling only if we assume a one-sided perspective: in particular, the perspective of the state from which the foreigner is smuggled out; as seen, instead, from the receiving state's perspective, as well as from an international perspective, this form of smuggling is not really different from the other, since in both cases the vectorial dynamic is that of a person who is helped out of a foreign country only to be helped enter another foreign country.

In Italian law, the crime of outbound smuggling was first introduced with l. 189/2002, modifying art. 12 TUIMM so as to criminalize, in sub-secs. 1 and 3, not only inbound smuggling, but also the conduct of anyone who performs "acts

24 See Procura della Repubblica di Palermo, Decreto di fermo, no. 615, 31.5.2017.

25 *Ibidem*.

directed to procuring the illegal entrance [of the foreigner] in a different state [than Italy] of which the person is not a citizen nor is entitled to permanent residency."[26] Arts. 4, sub-sec. 3, 22, sub-sec. 5 bis, letter a and 27 quater, sub-sec. 10, letter a, refer to this crime as "facilitation of clandestine emigration from Italy toward other states."

The reason why a crime of this kind exists is all but self-evident. From the perspective of both migratory policies and border defence, what states are directly concerned with is of course controlling entrance and presence of foreigners in their territory, not their exit. True, under certain conditions, states might be interested in certain numbers or certain categories of foreigners not leaving their territory; under current international law (as well as under current Italian law), however, they could not satisfy this interest by coercively preventing foreigners from departing or from being helped to depart. It is widely acknowledged, indeed, that persons have the right to leave every country, including their own (see, e.g., art. 16, sub-sec. 2, of the Italian Constitution and, above all, art. 12, sub-sec. 2, of the International Covenant on Civil and Political Rights, New York, 1966; henceforth: ICCPR). As a consequence, if we put aside certain exceptional cases (e.g., persons legitimately subjected to restrictive measures, such as detention, pre-trial detention, travel ban, etc.), exiting from the territory of a state is a perfectly legal conduct (or, at least, it should be so in signatory states to the ICCPR), which entails that helping them exit should not be criminalized either.[27]

If outbound smuggling is criminalized, this is only because, in a world totally subdivided into territorial sovereignties, exiting from the territory of a state necessarily entails, in practice, entering the territory of another state; and entrance into the territory of a foreign state (art. 12, sub-sec. 4, ICCPR) is not currently recognized to be a right, either by states or by international law.

Outbound smuggling, therefore, is itself, structurally, inbound smuggling, in the sense that what makes it a crime is not helping someone to exit from a foreign country but helping him or her to (irregularly) enter another foreign country. Nonetheless, the expression "outbound smuggling" can be usefully maintained, since it helps understand the fact that states criminalize

26 The linguistic incorrectness of this expression should be noticed: it is incorrect to say that "someone is entitled to permanent residency *of* a given state" (*avere titolo di residenza permanente* di *uno stato*); the correct expression is that someone is "entitled to permanent residency *in* a given state" (*titolo di residenza permanente* in *uno stato*), or, better still, that he or she "is a permanent resident of that state" (as the UNPS states).

27 In Italian law, this also entails that, according to sub-sec. 2 of art. 10 bis TUIMM, irregular foreigners who are found on their way to exiting the Italian territory cannot be charged with the crime of "clandestine immigration" established in sub-sec. 1 of the same article.

smuggling not only in their own interest, but also in the interest of other states. Inbound smuggling and outbound smuggling, in other words, express neatly different perspectives and principles: in the case of inbound smuggling, what is at stake is the territorial sovereignty of the state that criminalizes it, which is (allegedly) violated by the irregular entrance of foreigners into its territory; in the second case, instead, at stake are such principles as loyalty, solidarity and cooperation between states, which are relevant not only at the international level, but also, and even more, at the EU level. This is particularly true within the so-called Schengen area, in the context of which the criminalization of outbound smuggling can be seen as an implication of the right to free movement given to citizens of Schengen states.[28] Significantly, the Schengen Borders Code (6th Whereas) declares that "Border control is in the interest not only of the Member State at whose external borders it is carried out but of all Member States which have abolished internal border control. Border control should help to combat illegal immigration and trafficking in human beings and to prevent any threat to the Member States' internal security, public policy, public health and international relations."[29]

It is not by chance that the criminalization of outbound smuggling—in the form of facilitation of the foreigner's irregular transit through the territory of member states—is required by art. 1, sub-sec. 1, FD, according to which member states should criminalize "any person who intentionally assists a person who is not a national of a Member State to [...] *transit across* the territory of a Member State in breach of the laws of the State concerned on the [...] *transit* of aliens"; where it is clear that "entrance" and "transit" both refer to the same thing, as seen, however, from two different perspectives: in the first case, from the perspective of an overlapping between the state required to criminalize smuggling and the state in whose direct interest smuggling should be criminalized; in the second case, from the perspective of a separation between them.

On the other hand, the fact that outbound smuggling is not explicitly taken into account in the UNPS is not a coincidence either: the commitment to act in the immediate interest of another state can be conceived from a supranational viewpoint, such as the EU's, due to the interdependence of interests entailed in being part of such an overarching entity; an analogous commitment would instead be out of place from an international viewpoint, as is that of the UNPS,

28 Judges are thus right when they identify the founding reason of criminalizing outbound smuggling in the (assumed) "need for an international cooperation aimed at controlling and containing massive migratory fluxes, also in the spirit of the Schengen agreement." See, e.g., Cass., Sec. I, 6.10.2006, no. 34053; Cass., Sec. I, 13.5.2016, no. 9636.

29 Regulation (EC) No 562/2006, OJEU, 13.4.2006, L. 105, 6th Whereas.

even though it is informed by ideas of loyalty and cooperation between states parties.

1.4.4 *Some Phenomenological Features of Outbound Smuggling from Italy*

On a phenomenological level, we can begin by underlining that all cases of outbound smuggling from Italy are cases of overland smuggling. The reason is simple: outbound smuggling from Italy is basically linked to migrants' transit toward northern European countries (such as Germany, France, or the UK); it thus normally happens by crossing the land border between Italy and neighbouring states, such as France and Austria.[30] The observations concerning overland inbound smuggling which I made before are thus also applicable, in principle, to outbound smuggling.

Moreover, depending on the aim of the journey, two major forms of outbound smuggling can be distinguished: repatriation smuggling and transit smuggling. In the first case, the smuggler helps the foreigner, who finds himself or herself in Italy, to go back to his or her home country; since this country does not border on Italy, this entails that the foreigner is helped to go through the territory of (at least) a third state, of which he or she is neither a citizen nor a permanent resident; moreover, since the foreigner's home country is not a EU member state, this also entails that he or she has no right to move freely across the EU territory. In the second case, instead, the smuggler helps the foreigner to continue his or her journey toward its final destination, which is a different state than Italy.

After the crime was first introduced in 2002, many cases of repatriation smuggling were brought before the Italian courts, with citizens from such countries as Bulgaria, Latvia, Lithuania, Poland, Romania and Slovenia (which at that time were not yet in the EU), helped to leave Italy by irregularly entering the territory of neighbouring states—such as France or Austria—but then caught at the border, or just before crossing it.[31] Put on trial for outbound smuggling, their helpers objected that the aim of the foreigner's journey was not emigrating to the neighbouring state, but rather going through it with a view to returning to their home country.

From a literal point of view, this argument has no value at all: as we already know, the crime of outbound smuggling, according to art. 12, sub-secs. 1 and 3, only requires the performance of acts directed to procure the irregular entrance of a foreigner into the territory of a foreign state, whatever the aim or

30 See, e.g., Cass., Sec. I, 13.5.2016, no. 9636.

31 Cf. Angelo Caputo, 'I delitti di favoreggiamento delle migrazioni illegali', in Id. and Giorgio Fidelbo, *Reati in materia di immigrazione e di stupefacenti* (Giappichelli 2012) 69 ff.

duration of the entrance.[32] Even if we look at the supranational level, things are not very different: the FD, indeed, requires criminalization of "any person who intentionally assists a person who is not a national of a Member State [...] transit across[...] the territory of a Member State in breach of the laws of the State concerned on the [...] transit of aliens" (art. 1, sub-sec. 1, letter a), without distinguishing between transitory and durable transit.

Nevertheless, some judges have accepted the argument, maintaining, for instance, that criminalization of outbound smuggling is not aimed at protecting the formal intangibility of the Schengen area, but at fighting irregular immigration in, and emigration from, the state,[33] and that, starting from this assumption, no relevant harm is caused when "the transport is aimed at repatriation, by merely transiting through other states."[34]

1.4.5 *Inland Smuggling: Is Transnationality a Necessary Characteristic of the Crimes of Smuggling?*

The third basic legal form of the crime of smuggling is represented by (what I have already called) inland, or internal, smuggling. Its inclusion within the notion of migrant smuggling is generally undisputed, not only (as we will see shortly) in Italian law, but also at an inter- and supranational level. According to art. 6 UNPS, "Each State Party shall adopt such legislative and other measures as may be necessary to establish as criminal offences, when committed intentionally and in order to obtain, directly or indirectly, a financial or other material benefit: [...] Enabling a person who is not a national or a permanent resident to remain in the State concerned without complying with the necessary requirements for legally remaining in the State by [...] any [...] illegal means." On the other hand, art. 1, sub-sec. 1, FD requires "Each Member State" to "adopt appropriate sanctions on [...] any person who, for financial gain, intentionally assists a person who is not a national of a Member State to reside within the territory of a Member State in breach of the laws of the State concerned on the residence of aliens."

Italian law criminalises inland smuggling in art. 12, sub-sec. 5, TUIMM, as the action of "whoever, aiming at unfairly profiting either from a foreigner's condition of illegality or in connection with the activities punished according

---

32 So, indeed, Cass., Sec. I, 6.10.2006, no. 34053. Similarly: Cass., Sec. I, 25.1.2005, no. 4201; Cass., Sec. I, 20.1.2004, no. 3866; Cass., Sec. I, 5.12.2003, no. 5813; Cass., Sec. I, 2.12.2003, n. 492; Cass., Sec. I, 29.10.2003, no. 48838.

33 Cass., Sec. I, 26.10.2006, no. 42117.

34 Cass., Sec. I, 24.1.2006, no. 14545. Similarly: Cass., Sec. I, 7.4.2004, no. 18996; Cass., Sec. I, 27.1.2004, no. 12963; Cass., Sec. I, 22.10.2003, no. 45242; Cass., Sec. I, 7.10.2003, no. 8042 (arguing that "transiting in order to return to one's own country of origin" does not fall within the concept of "illegal entrance").

to this article, favours [the foreigner's] stay within the territory of the state in violation of the norms of this consolidated act." Such conduct, for instance, can take the form of hiring irregular foreigners,[35] or of providing them with accommodation.[36] This second kind of conduct has been, more recently,[37] made into a specific crime—let us call it *lodging smuggling*—which is defined, by sub-sec. 5 bis, as the action of "whoever, in return for payment, in order to obtain an unfair profit, provides accommodation [...] to a foreigner who does not have a residence permit." However, inland smuggling being a so-called free-form crime,[38] every contribution (even if consisting in a mere omission) made to the foreigner's irregular stay can amount to committing it.

However, two further conditions are necessary. First, as we will see later on (§ 1.6), the deed must be committed for profit. A second, negative, condition derives from the fact that, according to art. 12, sub-sec. 5, favouring a foreigner's irregular stay only amounts to the crime of internal smuggling "in circumstances falling outside the application of the previous sub-sections."[39] This means that the conduct of internal smuggling should not be part of the performance, by the same smuggler, of a wider sequence of actions that includes either inbound or outbound smuggling of the same foreigner. Relative to the crime of inbound smuggling, this entails, alternatively: 1) either that the foreigner's presence in the territory of the state is initially regular, only becoming irregular afterwards, as a consequence of the foreigner's overstaying his or her visa;[40] 2) or, if the foreigner's entrance was initially irregular, that the smuggler had not contributed to it, only limiting himself or herself to favouring the foreigner's stay. In any event, it is also required that the conduct of inland smuggling does not itself consist of acts directed to procuring the foreigner's irregular entrance into a third state, because otherwise the smuggler's conduct would amount to the crime of outbound smuggling, and favouring the foreigner's irregular stay would amount to a mere non-punishable *ante factum*.

Inland smuggling is thus opposed to both forms of cross-border smuggling due to its not requiring (or rather, to its requiring the absence of) a trans-border

35 E.g., Cass., Sec. III, 8.3.2001, no. 16064; Cass., Sec. I, 3.2.2004, no. 8065. In certain cases, however, it may be difficult to distinguish between internal smuggling under this form and the crime defined in art. 22, sub-sec. 12, as the action of a person who employs irregularly staying third-country nationals.

36 E.g., Cass. Sec. I, 16.10.2003, no. 46066; Cass., Sec. I, 23.10.2003, no. 46070.

37 With d.l. 92/98, converted into law by l. 125/98 and then modified by l. 94/2009.

38 Cass., Sec. I, 3.10.2006, no. 39952; Cass., Sec. I, 11.5.2005, no. 21049; Cass., Sec. III, 3.10.2006, no. 39952.

39 Analogously, sub-sec. 5 bis is only applicable "unless the act constitutes a more serious crime."

40 See, again, Cass., Sec. III, 3.10.2006, no. 39952.

movement of the foreigner. Because of this, though being generally acknowledged as a form of smuggling, it significantly impinges on many ideas currently circulating on this phenomenon. Above all, it challenges the idea that smuggling is—structurally, conceptually—a form of trans-border illegal transportation of persons and that, always entailing a violation of state territorial borders, it has a necessarily transnational character. Inland smuggling, indeed, lacks exactly this character, since the conduct in question both refers to subjects who already find themselves within the state territory (independently of their having entered either regularly or irregularly) and must not be aimed at helping them out of that same territory.

1.4.6 *Why Is Inland Smuggling Considered a Less Serious Crime than Cross-border Smuggling?*

From the point of view of Italian law, inland smuggling is less serious than cross-border smuggling. This is shown by many circumstances: firstly, and most obviously, by the sanctions respectively provided, which are higher in the case of cross-border smuggling[41] than in those of inland smuggling;[42] moreover, by the fact (see later on, § 1.6) that inland smuggling is only punished if committed for profit, whereas cross-border smuggling is punished independently from that aim; moreover, by the fact that the humanitarian defence in sub-sec. 2 only applies to cases in which the foreigners assisted already find themselves in the territory of the state, which excludes its applicability to inbound smuggling, while limiting it to cases of inland smuggling and outbound smuggling.

This different appraisal of the respective seriousness of different forms of smuggling is not easy to explain: in principle, the same reasons founding the punishment of cross-border smuggling also operate with regard to inland smuggling; in both cases, what seems to be at stake is, essentially, the need to control migratory fluxes on the state territory (as well as—secondarily and under certain conditions—the rights of the smuggled person: see later, § 1.8). Rather, from the perspective of a state concerned with avoiding

41 Art. 12, sub-sec. 1: imprisonment from one to five years and fine of 15,000 euros for every foreigner smuggled; sub-section 3: imprisonment from five to fifteen years and fine of 15,000 euros for every foreigner smuggled; sub-section 3 bis: further increase of the punishment established in sub-sec. 3 if more than one aggravating circumstances applies; sub-section 3 ter: imprisonment to be increased by one third to one half, and fine of 25,000 euros per foreigner smuggled, if conduct is committed either with the aim of exploitation or with the aim of profit.

42 Art. 12, sub-sec. 5: imprisonment up to four years and fine up to 15,493 euros overall, which can be increased by one third to one half if conduct either is committed by more than one person or concerns more than four persons; sub-sec. 5 bis: imprisonment from six months to three years and confiscation of the property used to accommodate the foreigner.

irregular immigration, the main problem should not be so much the momentary conduct of entrance, but the durable fact of staying; entrance should only have a secondary relevance, as an event after which the unwanted stay of the foreigner my occur: if entrance did not prelude a subsequent stay, there would be no reason for it to raise any problem from the perspective of the migratory policies of the state.

How, then, can we explain the fact that cross-border smuggling is considered a more serious crime than inland smuggling? A possible answer lies in the fact that only in the first case does the relevant conduct involve a violation of the state's territorial, physical, border, while in the other case the author does not determine *ex nihilo* this same violation, limiting himself or herself to consolidating, or to favouring, its consequences. Clearly, this is a formalistic explanation, attributing to the state the view that the main harm involved in migrant smuggling lies in the very fact of its borders being violated, and not so much—not primarily, at least—in the consequences that this "intrusion" might have in terms of control and management of foreign presences on its territory. If this explanation hits the mark, the main concern of the state in criminalizing migrant smuggling is the protection of its own "dignity", of its own territorial sovereignty seen as a macro-projection of its (alleged) right over its own "territorial body", of the state's sovereign right to decide from whom to be "penetrated."

To be clear, this does not mean that protection of the border only has a formalistic dimension: obviously, it is also linked to control and management of migratory fluxes. However, the fact that favouring irregular entrance is a more serious crime than favouring irregular stay seems to point in the direction of greater importance being given to the decision *in se* on who may cross the state's borders than to the claim to control and manage migration. This is confirmed, I argue, by the fact that inbound and outbound smuggling undergo the same legal treatment: what they share, indeed, is only violation of the border, while having instead opposite consequences in terms of unwanted presence of foreigners in the state's territory.

1.5 The Structure of Conduct

1.5.1 *Inbound Smuggling as a Typically Collective Crime?*

Besides being different from a vectorial viewpoint, as well as for their phenomenological features, different crimes of smuggling can also be distinguished, at a normative level, according to the way in which their conduct is structured.

Especially composite is, first of all, the description of the conduct of inbound smuggling. Both in sub-sec. 1 and in sub-sec. 3 of art. 12, it is organized around two different levels of definition: in their first part, both subsections indulge in an analytical enumeration of different forms that conduct can theoretically take on ("he or she who, in violation of this consolidated act, promotes, leads, organizes, finances or carries out the transportation of foreigners in the territory of the state"); then, in their second part, they both provide a synthetic open definition aimed at including other possible executive typologies ("or performs other acts aimed at procuring the [foreigner's] illegal entrance in the territory of the state"). This closing formula, as we will see, also refers to crimes of outbound smuggling, while the detailed enumeration in the first part only refers to inbound smuggling.

The point of this descriptive duplication, however, is not at all clear: in particular, it is not clear what use a detailed listing of possible forms of conduct can be, when the precision of such list is immediately frustrated by an all-encompassing closing formula.

Be that as it may, the analytical enumeration in the first part might, at most, count as a mere illustration aimed at pointing out that the most relevant manifestations of the crime are those committed by criminal organizations, resulting from joint criminal enterprises characterized by convergent complementary actions performed by different subjects with different roles (promoters, manager, organizers, financers, material executors [so-called *scafisti*]). This same kind of enumeration, indeed, can also be found in other norms explicitly criminalizing associative crimes, such as, for instance, art. 416 bis, sub-sec. 2, c.p., criminalizing "Those who promote, manage or organize" a mafia-type association; art. 270 c.p., criminalizing "Whoever, in the territory of the state, promotes, constitutes, organizes or manages [subversive] associations;" art. 270 bis c.p., criminalizing "Whoever promotes, constitutes, organizes, manages or finances [terrorist] associations."

Even thus interpreted, however, the enumeration remains completely useless in a practical perspective, completely devoid of any possible effect on either the norms' application or the amount of punishment to inflict.

1.5.2 *Crimes of Cross-border Smuggling as Inchoate Crimes: from Spatial to Aspirational Borders*

The second part of sub-secs. 1 and 3 contains, as was previously said, a brief and open description of the conduct of both forms of cross-border smuggling: there it is stated, indeed, that the crime is also committed when someone performs "other acts aimed at procuring the [foreigner's] illegal entrance either into the territory of the state or in the territory of another state, of which the person is neither a citizen nor a permanent resident." This way of describing the conduct of cross-border smuggling is peculiar to Italian law: it cannot be found, instead, in international sources. The peculiarity lies in the fact that the form of the crime actually committed does not require that the conduct be successful, that it effectively result in the "harm" sought to be prevented, i.e. the foreigner's irregular entrance in (or, in cases of outbound smuggling, his or her exit from) the territory of the state: it suffices, instead, that the smuggler commit acts directed to procuring the "harm"; in this sense, it can be said that the crimes of cross-border smuggling are construed, under Italian law, as crimes of mere action: they will be deemed as entirely committed (not merely attempted) independently of the attainment of the result, "for the sole reason that the agent, with his or her action, creates a condition, even an unnecessary one, teleologically linked to the potential illegal entrance of the foreigner in the territory of the state."[43] Cross-border smuggling falls, in other words, into the category of "substantive offences defined in the inchoate mode", which are "substantive offences defined in such a way as to penalize conduct before it reaches the stage of causing harm."[44] As such, they are instances of a so-called "anticipatory perspective on criminalization"[45] according to which the threshold of the complete crime is fixed at a moment in which it would ordinarily be relevant only as an attempted one:[46] that is, at a moment in which the agent, by performing substantial steps toward the procurement of the foreigner's irregular entrance (or exit), creates the risk that this result will effectively follow.[47]

The aim of this early criminalization is, evidently, that of widening as much as possible the protection of the state's territorial sovereignty, of its claim to have full control over its borders, due to the primary importance attributed to these same interests: as a result, the territorial borders of the state end up being indefinitely extended, from the perspective of their criminal law relevance, up to the point of being deterritorialized; they are thus protected not only against acts that violate them physically, but also against other acts that, though being committed far from them, are nonetheless animated by the aspiration to

---

43 Cf., among many others, Cass., Sec. I, 22.5.2014, no. 28819; Cass., Sec. I, 23.4.2015, no. 37277; Cass., Sec. I, 13.5.2016, no. 9636 (the latter specifically concerning a case of outbound smuggling).

44 For further general reflection on this category, see e.g. Andrew Ashworth and Lucia Zedner, *Preventive Justice* (Oxford University Press 2014) 97 ff.

45 See, on this concept, Jeremy Horder, 'Harmless Wrongdoing and the Anticipatory Perspective on Criminalization', in G.R. Sullivan and Ian H. Dennis (eds.), *Seeking Security: Pre-Empting the Commission of Criminal Harms* (Hart Publishing 2012) 79–102.

46 See, indeed, Ashworth and Zedner (n 44) 97: "The effect of defining an offence in [the inchoate mode] is that it occupies the existential space that the crime of attempt would otherwise have occupied."

47 Cf. Caputo (n 31) 45 ff.

violate them. In a way, it is as though the borders of the state stopped being linked to a material dimension, so as to assume a decidedly aspirational—thus essentially spiritual—dimension: as if they could be traced wherever there is someone actively aspiring to violate them.

This spiritualization of the border brings with it a corresponding spiritualization of the interest protected by the norm: apparently, what the criminalization of cross-border smuggling aims to protect is not the border materially understood, but rather—or, at least, first of all—the very idea of its impenetrability (or rather, selective penetrability). This goes hand in hand with what I have said before (§ 1.4.6) as to formalistic devotion to the idea of a border emerging from the fact that crimes of cross-border smuggling are deemed, under Italian law, to be more serious than those of inland smuggling.

Moreover, besides being troublesome from the perspective of the harm principle, this kind of anticipated criminalization also raises problems of vagueness (and is thus troublesome from the viewpoint of rule of law principles), since it makes the definition of the crime quite imprecise and risks expanding the area of punishability far beyond the limits of reasonableness: any act directed to producing the unwanted result can be relevant—hence punishable—as a crime of (cross-border) smuggling actually committed.

Such deviance from the fundamental principles of (Italian) criminal law is not at all supported by either inter- or supranational law, which do not require that smuggling crimes be defined in the inchoate mode. Art. 3 UNPS defines the concept of migrant smuggling (letter a) as "*the procurement*, in order to obtain, directly or indirectly, a financial or other material benefit, *of the illegal entry* of a person into a State Party of which the person is not a national or a permanent resident", then clarifying (letter b) that "Illegal entry" entails effectively "crossing borders." Art. 6, in its turn, requires criminalization of smuggling as thus defined, without calling for an inchoate construction of the crime. The FD does the same.

In truth, both instruments urge that smuggling also be punished in the attempted form (art. 6, sub-sec. 2, letter a, UNPS; art. 2 FD); however, as the UNPS expressly clarifies, each state is required to do so "Subject to the basic concepts of its legal system": and according to the "basic concepts" of Italian criminal law, the punishment of *acts directed* to committing smuggling would have derived in any case from the application of art. 56 c.p., as attempted smuggling, though with a lighter sentence than that applicable to the consummated form of the crime.[48]

48 See, however, Anne T. Gallagher and Fiona David, *The International Law of Migrant Smuggling* (Cambridge University Press 2014) 372, arguing that

According to an interpretation widely accepted by Italian judges, these difficulties have been allayed by the fact that, in the description of conduct, l. 189/2002 has substituted the original verb "favouring" with "procuring." This word is deemed to be more determined than the previous one;[49] the idea, in particular, is that, while directed to "favouring" could be said of any act aimed at facilitating or assisting the foreigner's entrance, at making it easier, directed to "procuring" could only be said of an act having the capacity to "cause" the (possible) result of the foreigner's irregular entrance.[50]

The difference between these two meanings seems to run parallel to that (not itself uncontroversial) between "causing" and "enabling", with the first entailing a more decisive contribution than the second: while directed to *favouring* (to *enabling*) the foreigner's entrance or transit could be any act making one of these results more probable, or easier, directed to *procuring* (to *causing*) them could only be an act which, other things being equal, makes their happening substantially certain.

1.5.3 *Inland Smuggling as a Resultative Crime*

These same kinds of interpretive troubles do not arise for crimes of inland smuggling, which are not construed as inchoate crimes, but as resultative crimes: their legal definition according to sub-secs. 5 and 5 bis does not revolve, indeed, around the performance of *acts directed to* procuring a given state of affairs; it requires, instead, that the author either successfully favours the foreigner's stay (sub-sec. 5) or, more specifically, provides accommodation

"It would run counter to the purpose of the Protocol if migrant smugglers, in this scenario,"—a scenario such as that to which I previously referred to as *smuggling interruptus*—"were able to avoid the most serious penalties by claiming they had merely *attempted* smuggling, rather than *succeeded* in completing the offense. There is nothing in the Protocol that requires States to differentiate between attempts and completed conduct. Instead, States are simply required to ensure that attempts are criminalized along with completed conduct. Given the potential for situations such as the ones described earlier in this paragraph, there may be practical benefits from a law enforcement and prosecution perspective to covering the entire smuggling process (from preparation, to attempt, to completed conduct) under one offense provision that allows for discretion in sentencing. This would also avoid the gaps that may follow efforts to break the smuggling process down into each and every one of its component parts."

In providing their interpretation, Gallagher and David heavily rely on the *Model Law against the Smuggling of Migrants* (UNODC 2010, available at: https://www.unodc.org/documents/human-trafficking/Model_Law_Smuggling_of_Migrants_10-52715_Ebook.pdf) 29.

49 However, this is not the way in which the concept of procurement is usually interpreted in the context of the UNPS: see Gallagher and David (n 48) 364–5.

50 Cf., e.g., Cass., Sec. III, 30.5.2012, no. 20880; Cass., Sec. I, 1.2.2013, no. 9816.

to him or her, which is *per se* a way of favouring his or her stay (sub-sec. 5 bis). Unlike crimes of cross-border smuggling, explicitly defined as crimes of mere action, independently of the actual occurrence of the relevant result (the foreigner's entrance or transit), crimes of internal smuggling are defined instead as revolving around the performance of a successful conduct: which entails that they require both that the effect of the foreigner's irregular stay effectively happen and that the smuggler's conduct contributes to it, even only to make it easier.[51]

1.5.4 *Rescuers and Mediated Smugglers: the Scope of Italian Criminal Jurisdiction*

The definition of cross-border smuggling as an inchoate crime affects the determination of the spatial ambit of application of the corresponding criminal norms, and therefore it also affects the spatial ambit of the Italian criminal jurisdiction.

A few years ago, Italian judges had to face (what they deemed to be) a legal conundrum created by what I have previously called *smuggling interruptus* (§ 1.4.1.2.1): smugglers (from both Libya and Egypt) frequently abandon the smuggled foreigners in the high seas on unseaworthy boats; if these foreigners are lucky, they either succeed in directly reaching the Italian shores or, more frequently, are rescued by private vessels (fishermen, NGOs) that are in the vicinity, or by the vessels of the state responsible for the corresponding SAR area. Subsequently they are brought to the nearest "place of safety" in Italy. This mode of execution entails that, while smugglers do perform acts directed to procuring the irregular entrance of foreigners in the Italian territory, they do not themselves physically enter that same territory: their conduct, from a material viewpoint, ends in the high waters.[52] The rest of the deed—including the foreigners' entrance into Italy—either is autonomously committed by the smuggled foreigners themselves or is determined by the decisive intervention of rescuers, who take charge of the migrants before their ship sinks.

According to Italian judges, this dynamic could raise problems as regards the applicability of Italian criminal law, and in particular of art. 12 TUIMM. Problems deriving from the fact that the fundamental principle governing the spatial validity of Italian criminal law is the principle of territoriality (arts. 3 and 6 c.p.), according to which Italian penal norms are applicable to deeds committed *within* the Italian territory.

51 Cf. Caputo (n 31) 77 ff.

52 Different, of course, is the case in which smugglers act in accord with subjects finding themselves in Italy. Cf., e.g., Cass., Sec. I, 23.6.2000, no. 4586.

More in detail, no problem is raised by those cases in which the smuggled foreigners themselves succeed in autonomously reaching the Italian shores, without resorting to rescuers' help: art. 6, sub-sec. 2, c.p. states indeed that "The crime is considered to have been committed in the territory of the state when [...] the event, which is the consequence of the criminal action, has happened therein." And this is clearly the case in our hypothesis, since the event (irregular entrance of foreigners) is a direct consequence of the smugglers' action—who organized the journey, provided the vessels and took the foreigners out to the high seas—without the intervention of any external factor interrupting the link between conduct and event.

More problematic, instead, is the case in which foreigners' entrance into Italy is a consequence of their being taken in charge by rescuers. What makes allegedly troublesome this typology of cases is the fact that the rescuers' intervention is a lawful—even dutiful—action, being imposed by norms of both national and international law: the International Convention for the Safety of Life at Sea (SOLAS, London, 1.11.1974, ratified by Italy with l. 313/1980), the International Convention on Maritime Search and Rescue (SAR, Hamburg, 27.4.1979, ratified by Italy with l. 147/1989), the UN Convention on the Law of the Sea (UNCLOS, Montego Bay, 10.12.1982, ratified by Italy with l. 689/1994), art. 1158 of the Italian navigation code (punishing—with up to two years of imprisonment—the captain of a vessel who omits to help persons in distress in those cases in which he or she has the duty to do so). Exactly because it is lawful/dutiful, it could be the case—this is the judges' interpretive anxiety—that the rescuers' intervention qualifies as a "supervening cause [...] able by itself to produce the event", to which art. 41, sub-sec. 2, c.p. acknowledges the effect of "excluding the causal relation" between criminal action and harmful event, and thus of excluding the possibility of imputing the latter to the author of the former. If this was the case, it would follow that, in these cases, the crime of inbound smuggling could not be deemed to have been committed in Italy according to art. 6 c.p., since the relevant event (foreigners' irregular entrance) could not be considered a consequence of smugglers' action—not at least in the legal sense expressed by art. 41 c.p. The territorial applicability of Italian criminal law would thus be ruled out. In the judges' view, this would also mean that Italian law could not be applied and that, consequently, the smugglers' deed could not be punished according to art. 12 TUIMM. (As I will show shortly, this last part of the argument is basically unfounded, so that the judges' interpretive effort aimed at overriding it is ultimately useless.)

Moreover, since the foreigners' entrance is a consequence of the rescuers' intervention, and since this intervention is lawful/dutiful, it could not be said that the entrance was "illegal", whereas art. 12 TUIMM defines cross-border smuggling exactly as the commission of acts aimed at "*illegally* procuring the [foreigners'] entrance into the state territory."

In order to avoid drawing the conclusion that smugglers could not be punished in cases of *smuggling interruptus* due to the fact that their conduct was entirely committed outside the Italian territory, judges have resorted to the dogmatic concept of "mediated author."[53] The argument goes approximately as follows: the rescuers' intervention in the high seas could not be considered a "cause by itself sufficient to procure the event" according to art. 41, sub-sec. 2, c.p., because it is not "an unforeseeable deed", being instead "not only foreseen, but also desired, even elicited. In sum, [...] the cynical action of abandoning" the migrants "in the high seas is exactly designed to create the situation of necessity stimulating" the rescuers' intervention, so as to obtain the foreigners' entrance into the territory of the state of destination. The rescuers' actions, thus, "should not be considered separately from the previous actions that determined the necessity to intervene, exactly because this is a situation of risk voluntarily caused by the smugglers." Their conduct is aimed at exploiting this situation; it should be thus considered as one and the same thing with both the necessity it provokes and the subsequent intervention to which this necessity gives rise. Though materially ending in the high seas, that conduct is ideally bound to the subsequent chain of events ending with the transportation of foreigners in a "place of safety" within the Italian territory: hence, while, from a material perspective, the rescuers' actions is the proximate cause of the foreigners' entrance into the state territory, the smugglers should be seen as the "mediated, indirect, authors" (i.e., as the *true* authors from a legal viewpoint) of that same result.[54]

This construction should make it possible to consider the deed as committed within the territory of the state according to art. 6 c.p. and, consequently, to apply art. 12 TUIMM: the foreigners' entrance, indeed, should be seen as illegal, even though it was materially due to an operation of rescue, since the rescuers' action should not be taken separately, but as part of the smugglers' criminal plan.

---

53 On which see, in general, Claus Roxin, *Täterschaft und Tatherrschaft* (7th edn., Walter de Gruyter & Co. 1999) ("Seither ist die Möglichkeit mittelbarer Täterschaft durch ein rechtmäßig handelndes Werkzeug allgemein anerkannt"). On the specific case of mediated authors acting through third persons' permissible conduct, see also Hartmut Johannes, *Mittelbare Täterschaft bei rechtmäßigem Handeln des Werkzeuges* (Klostermann 1963).

54 Cass., Sec. I, 28.2.2014, no. 14510.

In search of a firmer legal foundation, judges resort to art. 54 c.p., concerning the defence of necessity.[55] The rescuers' conduct—the argument goes—does not amount to a crime of inbound smuggling, not only because it is dutiful according to both domestic and international law, but also because it was committed in a state of necessity. According to art. 54, sub-sec. 3, however, "if the state of necessity was determined by another person's threat [...] the criminal responsibility for the deed should be attributed to the person who coerced the author to commit it," i.e. the so-called mediated author. This rule—in the judges' view—covers the smugglers' conduct which, while ending in the high seas, has nonetheless provoked the rescuers' intervention.

The anxieties underlying this complex judicial argumentation, however, are based on the incorrect assumption that, if we admit that the smugglers' conduct stopped in the high seas, the inapplicability of Italian criminal law (and thus, of art. 12 TUIMM) should follow. The mistake lies in an incomplete reconstruction of the rules governing the spatial validity of Italian criminal law. The principle of territoriality, indeed, as expressed in arts. 3 and 6 c.p., has an inclusive function, not an exclusive one: it is not aimed at establishing that Italian criminal law *only* applies to deeds committed in Italy, but that—"save for the exceptions established either by domestic public law or by international law" (art. 3, sub-sec. 1 c.p.: so-called "penal immunities")—it applies to *all* deeds committed in Italy. This does not mean, however, that it cannot also be applied, under given conditions, to deeds committed outside the Italian territory: on the contrary, this is expressly stated in sub-sec. 2 of art. 3, according to which "Italian law also obliges all those who, be they citizens or foreigners, find themselves abroad, though only in the specific cases determined either by Italian law itself or by international law." In these cases, the principle of territoriality is supplemented by other principles, which expand the scope of Italian criminal jurisdiction. The most relevant of these cases can be found listed in arts. 7 to 10 c.p. Among them, art. 10, sub-sec. 1, provides that "The foreigner who [...] commits abroad, to the harm of the state [...], a crime punished by Italian law with a minimum imprisonment of one year, shall be punished accordingly, if he or she finds himself or herself in the territory of the state and there is a request by the ministry of justice." This includes cross-border smuggling, which, on the one hand, is (conceived as) a crime against the state (that is, as harming such state interests as territorial sovereignty and

55 Cf., e.g., Cass., Sec. I, 1.2.2013, no. 9816; Cass., Sec. I, 28.2.2014, no. 14510; Cass., Sec. I, 23.5.2014, no. 36052; Trib. Catania, 20.2.2014 (available at https://www.unodc.org/res/cld/case-law-doc/criminalgroupcrimetype/ita/2014/proc__n__2932014_r_i_m_c_html/ITAh004_-_IT_293_2014_RIMC.pdf).

border control)[56] and, on the other hand, is punished by a minimum sentence of one year of imprisonment (1 to 8 years, in the case of sub-sec. 1; 5 to 15 years, in the case of sub-sec. 3).

According to general principles on the spatial validity of Italian criminal law, smuggling actions fall within art. 12 TUIMM even if they are entirely committed abroad, provided that they can be said to be *directed to procuring* irregular entrance of foreigners into the Italian territory. In order to obtain the same interpretive result, there is no need to resort to complex and uncertain dogmatic concepts such as the so-called "mediated author": it suffices that there be the ministry's request and that the smuggler, after committing the deed abroad, for whatever reasons finds himself or herself in Italy.

Further evidence in favour of this interpretation can be drawn from the consideration that it is exactly the need to fight against foreign criminals directing smuggling activities toward Italy from abroad that explains the criminalization of inbound smuggling in the inchoate mode.

1.6 Profit and No-profit Smuggling

Another distinction can be drawn between different legal configurations of smuggling, according to whether the smuggler's action, in order to be considered a crime, has to be performed for profit or not. Within Italian criminal law, this distinction runs parallel to that between cross-border (inbound or outbound) and inland smuggling. Unlike the UNPS, but in accord with the FD, indeed, art. 12 TUIMM, on the one hand, defines (both forms of) cross-border smuggling without requiring that conduct be performed for profit (i.e., that the actor be aiming at making money), while, on the other hand, establishing the profit aim requirement as an element of the crime of inland smuggling. Sub-secs. 1 and 3, in particular, do not even mention the aim of profit as an element of crime: cross-border smuggling is punishable even if it is performed for merely altruistic reasons, or for egoistic reasons different from economic enrichment. As we will see later on (§ 1.7), the aim of (directly or indirectly)[57]

56 See, e.g., Cass., Sec. I, 17.1.2017, no. 7416.

57 The accusation of an indirect aim of profit, consisting in publicity and international resonance, was originally made against the crew of the German humanitarian ship *Cap Anamur II*, in a case famously decided by the Tribunal of Agrigento about ten years ago: see Trib. Agrigento, 7.10.2009, no. 954 (available at http://www.meltingpot.org/IMG/pdf/tribunale_agrigento_15022010_1.pdf and http://www.meltingpot.org/IMG/pdf/tribunale_agrigento_15022010_2.pdf). For comments, see, among many others: Tugba Basaran, 'The saved and the drowned: Governing indifference in the name of security' [2016] Security

profiting from the deed is only taken into account, by sub-sec. 3 ter, letter b, as an aggravating factor of cross-border smuggling.

By contrast, inland smuggling is structurally defined as revolving around the aim of profit: as we know, the general form of the crime (sub-sec. 5) punishes "whoever, *in order to obtain an unfair profit from a foreigner's condition of illegality* [...], facilitates [the foreigner's irregular] stay" within the territory of the state; and the specific form of the crime, which I have called lodging smuggling (sub-sec. 5 bis), criminalises, in its turn, "whoever, *in return for payment, in order to obtain an unfair profit*, provides accommodation [...] to a foreigner who does not have a residence permit." However, there is no agreement among scholars as to the meaning to give to this "aim of unfair profit", nor do scholars agree as to whether the expression should be given the same meaning in both cases.[58] Older judicial decisions, for their part, were generally in agreement in maintaining that the "aim of unfair profit" element required, in both subsections, that the author acted with the intent to unjustly exploit the situation of the irregular foreigner, so as to make money by profiting from the weakness of his or her position before the law.[59] In more recent decisions, however, the idea tends to prevail that the unfair profit does not need to derive from a harm inflicted on the foreigner.[60]

I subscribe to the first judicial approach:[61] the expression in sub-sec. 5, "*in order to obtain an unfair profit from the foreigner's condition of illegality*", clearly entails, in my view, that the profit, at which conduct must be aimed: a) must be functionally, not occasionally, linked to the foreigner's irregular condition (which means that such profit could not be obtained if the same conduct was performed with regard to a person not in a "condition of illegality"); b) must be unfair exactly because of this same link. Under this perspective, the

---

Dialogue 211 ff.; Paolo Cuttitta 'Repoliticization Through Search and Rescue? Humanitarian NGOs and Migration Management in the Central Mediterranean' (2017) Geopolitics DOI: 10.1080/14650045.2017.1344834 (available at: https://www.tandfonline.com/doi/full/10.1080/14650045.2017.1344834); Sara Bellezza and Tiziana Calandrino, *Criminalization of Flight and Escape Aid* (borderline-europe 2017, available at: https://www.borderline-europe.de/sites/default/files/readingtips/Kidem%20final%20report%2005_2017.pdf).

58 See, e.g., among others, Massimo Donini, 'Il cittadino extracomunitario da *oggetto materiale* a *tipo d'autore* nel controllo penale dell'immigrazione' [2009] Questione giustizia 106 ff.; Caputo (n 31) 80 f., 86 ff.

59 E.g., Cass., Sec. III, 8.3.2001, no. 16064; Cass., Sec. I, 16.10.2003, no. 46066; Cass., Sec. I, 23.10.2003, no. 46070.

60 E.g., Cass., Sec. I, 2.2.2017, no. 32391. See also Cass., Sec. I, 2.2.2006, no. 5887.

61 See also Angelo Caputo, *Diritto e procedura penale dell'immigrazione* (Giappichelli 2006) 91 ff., 97 ff.; Gianni Bellagamba and Giuseppe Cariti, *La nuova disciplina dell'immigrazione* (Giuffrè 2008) 113, 116. *Contra*, however, Donini (n 58).

Italian approach to inland smuggling seems to be even more migrant-friendly than the UNPS: the latter indeed, as does the FD, only requires that conduct be performed with the aim of profit, but not that this aim consist in profiting from the foreigner's legal and social weakness due to his or her irregularity. Obtaining an unfair profit from the foreigner's irregular condition means taking advantage of this same condition, exploiting it, trying to draw economic benefits from it that could not be drawn if the foreigner was not in this condition: trying, in sum, to take advantage of the foreigner *as an irregular* subject. Something analogous can be said of lodging smuggling:[62] in the structure of sub-sec. 5 bis, the segments "in return for payment" and "in order to obtain an unfair profit" are clearly connected; this implies that, for the crime to be committed, an unfair profit has to derive exactly from the payment requested by the author of the foreigner; the unfairness of the former must be a function of the latter, which in turn entails that the unfairness of the profit must have its founding reason in corresponding unfairness of the payment, that is, in imposing unfairly burdensome contractual conditions on the irregular foreigner, thus taking advantage of the irregular condition that makes him or her an extremely weak contractual party.

1.6.1 *Rescue and Humanitarian Smuggling*

From no-profit smuggling (that is, smuggling not committed with the aim to make money) we should distinguish (what we could dub) rescue and humanitarian smuggling (that is, helping foreigners to unorthodoxly[63] enter or stay in the territory of the state in order to either rescue them from situations of need or provide them with humanitarian assistance).[64]

---

62 See also Luca Masera, 'Immigrazione', in Oliviero Mazza and Francesco Viganò (eds.), *Misure urgenti in materia di sicurezza pubblica* (Giappichelli 2008) 21 ff. *Contra*, again, Donini (n 58).

63 I here prefer to use this unusual expression, instead of the usual concept of "irregular" entrance or stay, because, in the cases to which I will be referring in this excursus, it is not at all clear whether the foreigner's entrance and permanence can be properly deemed "irregular." By defining them merely "unorthodox", I mean that they take place in different forms than those established as canonical, as normal and appropriate, by the law (e.g., entrance through specific border crossing points [art 4 TUIMM] or residence permit renewal [art. 5 TUIMM]), but, nonetheless, under closer inspection, they may turn out to be, all things considered, not irregular, not in violation of the law.

64 On humanitarian smuggling, see, among others, Rachel Landry, 'Decriminalising 'Humanitarian Smuggling' (2017) 6 RSC Research in Brief (available at https://www.rsc.ox.ac.uk/publications/research-in-brief-decriminalising-humanitarian-smuggling/@@download/file); Cuttitta (n 57). With specific regard to the French criminalization of a so-called *délit de solidarité*, see Jennifer Allsopp, 'Contesting *fraternité*. Vulnerable migrants

It is unclear whether and to what extent rescue and humanitarian smuggling can be classified as smuggling in the proper sense. Undoubtedly, smuggling cannot be deemed to be committed in those cases in which transporting irregular foreigners or helping them to stay in the Italian territory are consequences of saving them from situations of serious and imminent danger for their physical integrity or life: in these cases, indeed, conduct is either the content of a specific duty (as happens in many hypotheses of rescue at sea: see above, § 1.5.4) or, in any event, is covered by the justification defence of necessity, which, as we have seen, Italian law considers in art. 54 c.p., by establishing that "He or she should not be punished who was compelled to commit the deed by the necessity to save either himself or herself or another person from the imminent danger of a serious personal harm, a danger not voluntarily determined by himself or herself, nor otherwise avoidable, and provided that the deed is proportioned to the danger" (art. 54, sub-sec. 1). When these conditions apply, the entrance and the stay of the foreigner cannot be said to be illegally procured, which radically excludes the possibility of qualifying the deed as one of smuggling.

Problems arise, instead, in those cases in which rescuers do not act out of strict necessity and absolute emergency: cases in which foreigners are not properly saved from a serious and imminent danger for their life or personal integrity, but either find themselves in a more generic state of need (difficult health conditions requiring significant but not life-saving intervention, food deprivation not amounting to starving, etc.) or are escaping from "man-made disasters, including armed conflict, or natural disasters."[65]

Italian law considers such hypotheses in sub-sec. 2 of art. 12 TUIMM, by establishing that "Without prejudice to art. 54 of the penal code, rescue and humanitarian assistance do not amount to crimes insofar as they are provided *in Italy* to foreigners in need who find themselves, even if irregularly, *within the territory of the state*." As can easily be grasped, this disposition can only be applied to cases of either inland or outbound smuggling, since it is only in these cases that rescued/assisted foreigners already find themselves in the Italian

---

and the politics of protection in contemporary France' [2012] RSC Working Paper Series (available at: https://www.rsc.ox.ac.uk/files/files-1/wp82-contesting-fraternite-2012.pdf).

65 "Notwithstanding differing terminology, "humanitarian assistance" thus comprises providing goods and services essential for the survival of those being directly affected by man-made disasters, including armed conflict, or natural disasters. It may comprise material aid and/or the services of personnel" [Heike Spieker, 'The Right to Give and Receive Humanitarian Assistance', in Hans-Joachim Heintze, Andrej Zwitter (eds.), *International Law and Humanitarian Assistance. A Crosscut Through Legal Issues Pertaining to Humanitarianism* (Springer 2011) 7].

territory. Conduct of inbound smuggling, referring necessarily to foreigners who have not already entered the state territory, is instead excluded from the range of application of the defence; this entails that criminal responsibility for inbound smuggling can only be excluded if the general conditions either of art. 54 c.p. or of duty of rescue apply (a duty that, in its turn, does not stem from the foreigner's mere need of humanitarian assistance, given that this need, while founding claims against states,[66] does not found *per se* any claim against individuals.)

This limitation is clearly aimed at circumscribing as much as possible the number of cases in which helping foreigners to unorthodoxly enter the state territory can be deemed to be lawful.

In any event, whatever its axiological foundation may be, this same limitation is technically questionable; its effect, indeed, is an almost complete redundancy of the norm in art. 12, sub-sec. 2, TUIMM: that inland smuggling is not punishable if committed for reasons of rescue and humanitarian assistance stems directly from the definition of the crime given by sub-secs. 5 and 5 bis, which, as we have previously seen, requires that conduct be performed for profit. The disposition in sub-sec. 2 is thus practically relevant only for cases of outbound smuggling.[67]

A quick comparison with both supranational and international law confirms these perplexities. As previously said, the Italian definition of inland smuggling aligns itself much more with the FD (only establishing the aim of "financial gain" as a constitutive element of inland smuggling, but not of cross-border smuggling) than with the UNPS (which instead establishes the aim of profit as a definitional element of all forms of smuggling). Curiously, however, the way followed by Italian law as regards the (limited) relevance of the humanitarian factor is almost opposite to that suggested in the FD: the latter, indeed, in art. 1, sub-sec. 2, limits the (possible, not necessary) relevance of the humanitarian factor to cases defined in sub-sec. 1, letter a, that is to *all* cases of cross-border smuggling, while not referring it to cases in letter b (inland smuggling).[68] This makes sense: if we start from the assumption—which in

66 Spieker (n 65) 8 ff.

67 See, e.g., Trib. Imperia, 27.4.2017, no. 446, applying the defence (though only in the putative form: art. 59, sub-sec. 4, c.p.) to Felix Croft, a French activist who tried to smuggle a Sudanese family (coming from Darfur) from the Italian city of Ventimiglia to France, being convinced that they needed humanitarian assistance and that the only way to provide them with it was taking them to his home.

68 "Any Member State may decide not to impose sanctions with regard to the behaviour defined in paragraph 1(a) by applying its national law and practice for cases where the aim of the behaviour is to provide humanitarian assistance to the person concerned."

principle I find reasonable—that aim of profit and humanitarian aim are mutually exclusive, the non-punishability of inland smuggling if committed with "the aim [...] to provide humanitarian assistance" can already be inferred, *a contrario*, from this crime being defined as a crime of profit ("any person who, *for financial gain*, intentionally assists etc."). It is instead with regard to cases of cross-border smuggling (which are criminalized even if not committed for profit) that a humanitarian defence makes sense (i.e., is not redundant).

The same assumption—that aim of profit and humanitarian aim are incompatible—also helps explain why, instead, there is no mention of humanitarian defence in the UNPS: such defence would be completely redundant in this case exactly because, in the UNPS, the aim "to obtain, directly or indirectly, a financial or other material benefit" is established, in art. 6, as a general requirement for criminalization of (any form of) smuggling. And indeed, according to the Interpretive notes for the official records (travaux préparatoires) of the negotiation of the United Nations Conventions against Transnational Organized Crime and the Protocols thereto, the fact that the smuggler's aim of getting some material benefit from his conduct is a definitional element of the crime excludes from the scope of criminalisation "the activities of those who provided support to migrants for humanitarian reasons or on the basis of close family ties."[69]

1.6.2 *NGOs as Humanitarian Smugglers? the Luventa Case*

The irrelevance of a humanitarian aim with respect to inbound smuggling underlies some recent cases in which the crew of some NGO ships have been charged with this crime. The argument was, in particular (but the cases are still on trial), that some of these ships did more than just rescuing foreigners at sea, to the point of establishing forms of cooperation with the smugglers, who ended up relying on their intervention as one of the factors on the basis of which to organize their criminal activity.

It is interesting here to take such hypotheses into consideration in order to see whether and to what extent criminal norms against smuggling can be applied to them. As we have seen (above, § 1.4.2.1.1), one of the most frequent ways of committing the crime along the central Mediterranean routes is smuggling interruptus. As regards the responsibility of private ships (such as the

69 United Nations—General Assembly, 'Interpretive notes for the official records (travaux préparatoires) of the negotiation of the United Nations Conventions against Transnational Organized Crime and the Protocols thereto' [2000] A/55/383/Add. 1, § 88 (but see also § 92). See also Gallagher and David (n 48) 366.

NGOs') helping migrants abandoned by smugglers in the high seas, it is possible to distinguish two fundamental scenarios.

First, one can suppose that no agreement exists between smugglers and NGOs; smugglers may, of course, know that NGO ships find themselves in the high seas with the specific mission of helping smuggled foreigners, and they may also take advantage of this knowledge so as to organize their activity accordingly; it cannot be said, however, that the NGOs themselves voluntarily participated in planning these activities with the smugglers; they limit themselves to a completely lawful—if not dutiful—rescue intervention and could not be charged with inbound smuggling; in effect, it is exactly the lawfulness of their intervention that, as we have seen (above, § 1.5.4), has raised some interpretive problems as to the applicability of Italian criminal law even to the smugglers' conduct. Importantly, the lawfulness of the NGOs' conduct is not affected by their being aware of the fact that smugglers use their presence as part and parcel of their criminal project: reciprocal awareness does not amount to an agreement, at least insofar as the NGOs can reasonably suppose that, even in absence of their intervention, the smugglers would all the same have abandoned the foreigners in the high seas.

Things change, however, if we suppose (and this is the second scenario) that there is some kind of (not necessarily explicit) agreement between smugglers and NGOs, according to which a certain number of migrants are consigned in the high seas by the former to the latter in order to be brought to Italy under the appearance of a rescue operation. This is the accusation recently made against the crew of the *Iuventa*, a vessel flying the flag of the Netherlands but belonging to the German NGO Jugend Rettet. According to the g.i.p. of Trapani,[70] the *Iuventa* crew were used to meeting smugglers' in the high seas (but sometimes even in the Libyan territorial sea) and taking on board the migrants that the smugglers had previously crammed in son ships following their mothership; the crew were also used not to destroying these same ships after the transhipment, in violation of the orders held by the Italian Maritime Rescue Coordination Centre; on at least some of these occasions, an "agreed delivery of migrants" is supposed to have taken place, in the absence of an immediate danger necessitating a rescue operation under the Montego Bay convention; moreover, according to the g.i.p., the fact that, at the end of the transhipment operations, the boats and dinghies used by the smugglers as son ships were not destroyed but returned to them (in order to be re-used for subsequent journeys) should be seen as irrefutable evidence of the fact that the aim of the *Iuventa* crew was not limiting themselves to mere rescue, but instead creating a

70 G.i.p. Trapani, Decree of preventive seizure, no. 816, 2.8.2017.

preferential and fiduciary relationship with the smugglers so as to favour their further activities of illegal immigration. This aim is deemed, by the g.i.p., sufficient to amount to the *mens rea* of the crime of inbound smuggling, because it entails that "the crew of the *Iuventa* were perfectly aware of both violating Italian law on immigration and helping the smugglers' business." Nonetheless, the g.i.p. also maintains that the crew were acting out of humanitarian reasons, and that, because of this, they should not be charged with being participants in the Libyan smugglers' criminal organization. This is a crucial point for us: as the judge argues, "it is clear [...] that the NGOs' aims are diametrically opposite to those of the smugglers' criminal organization; while the latter aims at exploiting the weak position of subjects aspiring to leave their countries as a way of making money, the NGOs aim instead at facilitating the migrants' aspiration to leave Africa, which is completely in their favour." The *Iuventa* crew, as a consequence, is not charged with being part of the Libyan criminal organization aimed at smuggling, but with complicity in specific acts of smuggling.

Now, whatever the validity of these charges in the concrete case, the scenario emerging from what has been said so far outlines a paradigmatic hypothesis of humanitarian smuggling: by acting in complicity with the smugglers, the NGO vessels' crew commit acts directed to procuring the irregular entrance of foreigners into the Italian territory; these acts—let us assume it for the sake of argument—do not serve to rescue foreigners from imminent danger, being based instead on agreed deliveries; however, this conduct is performed for humanitarian purposes. As we have seen, under current Italian law, insofar as they are disconnected from a situation of imminent danger for foreigners' lives or physical integrity, these purposes are no defence against the charge of inbound smuggling. The sole possibility of acquitting these NGO crews on humanitarian grounds would be applying analogically the defence in art. 12, sub-sec. 2, so as to extend it to cases of inbound smuggling. Though there have been scholars suggesting a similar interpretation,[71] it is extremely improbable that it is going to have some kind of appeal for judges, given the general "political climate" of increasing suspiciousness as regards NGOs' activities in the Mediterranean sea. The only other option remaining is the application of the (general) attenuation factor established in art. 62, no. 1, c.p., according to which a more lenient punishment should be inflicted on those who commit a crime for highly praiseworthy human and social reasons.[72]

71 E.g., Caputo (n 34) 93–4.

72 See, indeed, G.i.p. Trapani (n 70).

1.7 Basic and Aggravated Forms of Smuggling

Those analysed so far represent the basic forms of smuggling. Sub-sections 3, 3 ter and 5 (second part) of art. 12 establish its aggravated forms.

Sub-sec. 3, in particular, establishes that a more severe punishment must be inflicted when the commission of one of the deeds referred to in sub-sec. 1 is accompanied by any of the following circumstances: "a) the deed concerns the entrance or the stay of five or more persons in the territory of the state; b) in order to procure his or her entrance or stay, the life or the physical integrity of the person transported was exposed to risk; c) in order to procure his or her entrance or stay, the person transported was subjected to inhuman or degrading treatment; d) the deed was committed by three or more persons acting together, or by resorting to international services of transportation, or by using counterfeited, or illegally obtained, documents; e) the authors of the deed had either arms or explosives at their disposal." Moreover, according to sub-sec. 3 ter, punishment should be further increased in severity if the deeds referred to in sub-secs. 1 or 3 "a) are committed with a view to recruiting persons for purposes of prostitution or for other forms of either sexual or work exploitation, or [if those deeds] concern the entrance of minors to employ in illicit activities in order to favour their exploitation; b) are committed with an aim of (direct or indirect) profit."

Without going into detail about these hypotheses, it suffices to say, in general, that the aggravating factors thereby established appear to be inspired by three different fundamental concerns. In some cases, the aggravation is due to the fact that the crime is deemed especially harmful (because of the high number—five or more—of foreigners smuggled in); other circumstances, instead, are deemed to show particular insidiousness or dangerousness of the authors (because of their acting in a group, or because of their using counterfeited documents or international transport services, or because of their bringing arms and explosives with them). In still other cases, the aggravation is made dependent upon the fact that the concrete execution of the crime causes harm to the smuggled foreigner: this is clearly the case for the aggravating factors in letters b and c of sub-sec. 3 (revolving respectively around the endangerment of the lives or safety of the smuggled migrants and their being inhumanly or degradingly treated); but it is also the case for those in sub-sec. 3 ter, both concerning the exploitation of smuggled foreigners (either as "labour" for prostitution, irregular work or other illegal activities, or as sources of direct or indirect enrichment).

Some of these aggravating factors are also considered in inter- or supranational legal instruments. According to art. 6, sub-sec. 3 UNPS, for instance,

"Each State Party shall adopt such legislative and other measures as may be necessary to establish as aggravating circumstances to the offences established in accordance with paragraph 1 (a), (b) (i) and (c) of this article and, subject to the basic concepts of its legal system, to the offences established in accordance with paragraph 2 (b) and (c) of this article, circumstances: (*a*) That endanger, or are likely to endanger, the lives or safety of the migrants concerned; or (*b*) That entail inhuman or degrading treatment, including for exploitation, of such migrants."[73] On the other hand, according to art. 1, sub-sec. 3 FFD, "Each Member State shall take the measures necessary to ensure that, when committed for financial gain, the infringements defined in Article 1(1)(a) and, to the extent relevant, Article 2(a) of Directive 2002/90/EC are punishable by custodial sentences with a maximum sentence of not less than eight years where they are committed in any of the following circumstances: [...]—the offence was committed while endangering the lives of the persons who are the subject of the offence."

Lastly, with regard to the crime of inland smuggling, the second part of sub-sec. 5 establishes that a more severe punishment should be inflicted "When the deed is committed by two or more persons acting together, or when it concerns the stay of five persons or more." As can be easily inferred, these circumstances reproduce those respectively established—with regard to cases of cross-border smuggling—in letters d (first part) and a of sub-sec. 3. Nothing is said, however, as to cases in which, while being objects of inland smuggling, foreigners are, for instance, treated inhumanly or degradingly or their life or physical integrity is put at risk.

1.8 Why Punish Migrant Smuggling?[74]

Having both reconstructed the general features of the Italian criminal approach to migrant smuggling and compared them with those emerging from inter- and supranational sources, and also having identified some of the most significant criminological features of the phenomenon, it is now time to question why states are so eager to counter it. There are two main answers to this. The first has to do with migrant smuggling being linked to irregular immigration:

73 Cf. Gallagher and David (n 48) 374 ff.

74 The paragraphs from 1.8.1 to 1.8.2 are based on what I have previously written in Alessandro Spena, 'Human smuggling and irregular immigration in the EU: from complicity to exploitation?', in Sergio Carrera, Elspeth Guild (eds.), *Irregular migration, trafficking and smuggling of human beings. Policy dilemmas in the EU* (CEPS 2016) 33 ff.

although it should be clear that not all smuggled migrants are irregular in the proper sense (many of them being refugees and asylum seekers), smuggling is nonetheless one of the most eye-catching ways (at least for the mass media) by which irregular immigration takes place; fighting it can thus be a way of fighting irregular immigration itself. Smuggled migrants are given an unclear role under this approach: while, on the one hand, they are not necessarily to be criminalised for the mere fact of having been smuggled, on the other hand, it is clear that their rights and needs are not what states are fighting for when they adopt this perspective. In a sense, migrants are rather part of the problem that is ultimately addressed by fighting smuggling.

The second reason why states may be particularly concerned with human smuggling stems, instead, from the need to protect the migrants themselves from the many risks they may face if smuggled: economic exploitation, deception, degrading treatment along the way, death, and so on.[75] Under this approach,[76] smuggled migrants will probably be perceived, to a certain extent, as victims—either of the smugglers who thrive on their aspiration to go abroad or of the (political, economic, climatic) situations due to which they decide to migrate by entrusting themselves to smugglers.[77]

---

75 On these risks, see, e.g. *Smuggling of migrants into, through and from North Africa* (UNODC 2010, available at: www.unodc.org/documents/human-trafficking/Migrant_smuggling_in_North_Africa_June_2010_ebook_E_09-87293.pdf) Ch. IX; Philippe De Bruycker, Anna Di Bartolomeo and Philippe Fargues, 'Migrant smuggled by sea to the EU: Facts, laws and policy options' (2013) 9 MPC Research Report (available at: http://www.migrationpolicycentre.eu/docs/MPC-RR-2013-009.pdf) 4 ff.; *Smuggled Futures: The dangerous path of a migrant from Africa to Europe, Geneva: Global Initiative against Transnational Organised Crime* (Global Initiative against Transnational Organised Crime 2014, available at: www.globalinitiative.net/smuggled-futures/) 7 ff.

76 See, e.g., Tom Obokata, 'Smuggling of Human Beings from a Human Rights Perspective: Obligations of Non-State and State Actors under International Human Rights Law' [2005] International Journal of Refugee Law 394–415; Matilde Ventrella, 'Recognizing Effective Legal Protection to People Smuggled at Sea, by Reviewing the EU Legal Framework on Human Trafficking and Solidarity between Member States' [2015] Social Inclusion 76–87.

77 There may be also a third reason for states to criminalise migrant smuggling, which however is not based so much on a structural, necessary feature of the crime, but on one of its possible criminological dimensions: this dimension is linked to the significant role frequently played by criminal organizations in the business of migrant smuggling. Criminalising this activity may thus be a way for states to strengthen their armoury in the fight against organized crime. This third perspective, however, is not alternative to the other two; it more properly overlaps with them, according to whether the presence of organized crime in the business of migrant smuggling is seen as a threat for state interests (its territorial sovereignty, including its ability to establish itself as the monopolist of the legitimate use of force within its territory), for the rights of the smuggled persons (the right not to be exploited, the right not to have their lives put in danger, etc.) or for both:

1.8.1 *The EU Approach: Smuggling as Complicity in Irregular Migration*

The EU law against migrant smuggling so far has been strongly dominated by the aim to fight irregular migration.[78]

The key legislative pieces in this field, the FFD and the FD,[79] do not even speak of "(migrant) smuggling", but of "facilitation of irregular migration", which displays from the very beginning the fact that the focus here is not so much on smuggled migrants as objects or victims of a crime as on their being authors of the conduct that is ultimately to be prevented, i.e. irregular migration.

Accordingly, art. 1 FD makes the definition of the "general infringement" of facilitation revolve around the conduct of "assisting" irregular immigrants either to enter, or transit across, (art. 1, sub-sec. 1, letter a) or to stay in (art. 1, sub-sec. 1, letter b) the territory of a member state, which clearly shows that, in the FD perspective, human smuggling's wrongness is seen as lying in its being a help to migrants who aspire to irregularly migrate to the EU. This becomes even more clear if we consider that, as already mentioned earlier (see above, § 1.6), as regards the conduct of facilitation of entrance, the definition of the offence does not even require the facilitator to act "for financial gain" (as is required, instead, in the case of facilitation of stay), which apparently entails that the independent moral content of the facilitator's conduct is of secondary importance to the definition of what is wrong with smuggling from the EU's point of view.

In other words, although irregular migration is not directly criminalised either in the FD or in the FFD, it is nonetheless this conduct that is seen as expressing the core wrongness at stake here. Paradoxical as it may seem, in the FD's approach, smuggling, as a form of facilitation, is only wrongful in an ancillary way, as if it was only a form of complicity in the real wrong, which is the wrong of irregular migration.

A "complicity approach" to smuggling is the logical consequence of the EU's general approach to migration during the last few years, which has been basically driven, at least at the level of political declarations, by the need to secure the EU's external borders as a countermeasure for having opened the internal

---

the association of organized crime with migrant smuggling, in other words, does not provide states with an independent reason to criminalise migrant smuggling, nor provides them with an independent reason to criminalise organized crime; it merely reinforces the reasons they already have to fight against the one as well as the other with reference to the cases in which the two phenomena intersect.

78 See, e.g., Valsamis Mitsilegas, *The Criminalization of Migration in Europe. Challenges for Human Rights and the Rule of Law* (Springer 2015) 52 ff.

79 On which see, among others, Mitsilegas (n 78); Gallagher and David (n 48) 89 ff., 393 ff.

borders between member states.[80] This has led to a veritable obsession with the fight against irregular migration: an obsession of which the EU's way of fighting smuggling is a corollary.

1.8.1.1 The Rights of the Smuggled Persons in EU Law

EU law, of course, does not completely disregard the rights of smuggled migrants; it could not do so, since many of these rights are either expressly recognised in the EU Charter of Fundamental Rights or are the object of international obligations for the member states.[81] My point is, however, that EU law does not pay these rights the attention they deserve.

Two examples. We already know that, according to art. 1, sub-sec. 2, "Any member state may decide not to impose sanctions with regard to the behaviour defined in paragraph 1(a) by applying its national law and practice for cases where the aim of the behaviour is to provide humanitarian assistance to the person concerned." Behind this apparently *in bonam partem* provision, there lies a clue to the fact that humanitarian concerns are not a key worry for EU law against smuggling. The meaning of art. 1, sub-sec. 2, is, indeed, that member states are not obliged, but merely permitted to grant "facilitators" a humanitarian defence for their conduct. In member states that avail themselves of this possibility not to grant a humanitarian defence for smuggling (as for instance Italy does with regard to cross-border smuggling: see above, § 1.6.1), this raises significant risks for potential helpers of being criminalised as smugglers, thereby indirectly impinging upon the chances migrants have to be helped when they find themselves in need of humanitarian assistance.[82]

---

80 See, e.g., European Parliament and Council, *Regulation (EC) No 562/2006 of 15 March 2006 establishing a Community Code on the rules governing the movement of persons across borders (Schengen Borders Code)*, OJ L 105, 13.4.2006.

81 Obokata (n 76) 400 ff.

82 In general, on the risk of being criminalised faced by humanitarian helpers, see, e.g., Elspeth Guild and Sergio Carrera (2013), 'EU Borders and Their Controls. Preventing unwanted movement of people in Europe?' [2013] CEPS Essay (available at: https://www.ceps.eu/system/files/No%206%20EU%20Borders%20and%20their%20Controls%20revised.pdf) 2 (underscoring "the role of current EU anti-smuggling and trafficking legislation and the way it has been transposed into national law by EU member states, which often creates a presumption that a captain is committing the offence of smuggling or trafficking if he or she brings unauthorized people into harbours. The consequence is criminal prosecution and confiscation of the individual's boat"); Jennifer Allsopp, 'The European Facilitation Directive and the Criminalisation of Humanitarian Assistance to Irregular Migrants: Measuring the Impact on the Whole Community', in Sergio Carrera, Elspeth Guild (eds.), *Irregular migration, trafficking and smuggling of human beings. Policy dilemmas in the EU* (CEPS 2016) 47. See also Basaran (n 57) 205, arguing that public

Another telling example is art. 1, sub-sec. 3, second indent, of the FFD, which requires member states to punish facilitation of entry (as well as, "to the extent relevant", the conduct defined in art. 2, letter a FD) more severely if committed "while endangering the lives of the persons who are the subject of the offence." This shows, again, that insufficient attention is paid to immigrants' rights: why indeed limit the scope of this aggravated responsibility to the fact that migrants' lives are put at risk, hence overlooking the relevance of many other ways in which migrants can be victimised during the smuggling process (exploitation, deception, extortion, maltreatment)?[83]

1.8.1.2 The EU Action Plan against Migrant Smuggling (2015–2020)

In the EU Action Plan against Migrant Smuggling (2015–2020),[84] published in May 2015, the European Commission announced, among other things, that it "will make, in 2016, proposals to improve the existing EU legal framework to tackle migrant smuggling which defines the offence of facilitation of unauthorized entry and residence, and strengthen the penal framework. It will seek to ensure that appropriate criminal sanctions are in place while avoiding risks of criminalisation of those who provide humanitarian assistance to migrants in distress."

The Commission seemed thus to be ready to abandon the "complicity approach" to human smuggling, with smugglers not depicted as mere migrants' facilitators anymore, but rather as exploiters of their vulnerability ("Smugglers treat migrants as goods, similar to the drugs and firearms that they traffic along the same routes"), jeopardising their lives and human rights in order to obtain material gains (smugglers "make substantial gains while putting migrants' lives at risk. To maximize their profits, smugglers often squeeze hundreds of migrants onto unseaworthy boats—including small inflatable boats or end-of-life cargo ships—or into trucks. Scores of migrants drown at sea, suffocate in containers or perish in deserts. […] The human rights of migrants are often gravely violated through abuse and exploitation").

Unfortunately, the implementation of the Plan so far has limited itself to police and operational aspects; the announced "revision of EU legislation on migrant smuggling by 2016" has not taken place. As a consequence, the EU approach on the criminalisation of smuggling, as well as its view on the role of

policies criminalizing actions of rescue are inducing collective indifference toward people drowning at sea in the name of security.

83 See, again, Obokata (n 76) 400 ff.

84 European Commission, 'EU Action Plan against Migrant Smuggling (2015–2020)', COM(2015) 285 final, Brussels, 27.05.2015.

smuggled migrants, today continue to be same as those shaped, sixteen years ago, by the FD and the FFD.

1.8.2 *The UN Approach: Smuggling as Exploitation*

The UN approach to human smuggling, as it emerges from the UNPS,[85] is considerably different from that of the EU: not only because it is explicitly concerned with migrant smuggling as a way to combat transnational organized crime, but—and this is more interesting for us here—because of the relevance it gives to smuggled migrants' rights. Indeed, though they are not formally qualified as victims,[86] the protection of their rights is among the Protocol's main concerns, as is explicitly stated, for example, in art. 2: "The purpose of this Protocol is to prevent and combat the smuggling of migrants, as well as to promote cooperation among states Parties to that end, while protecting the rights of smuggled migrants."[87] Accordingly, the general definition of the offence in the UNPS is not framed in terms of "complicity" ("help", "assistance") in the immigrants' conduct (as it is in the FD), but as "the procurement [...] of the illegal entry of a person into a state Party of which the person is not a national or a permanent resident" (art. 3, letter a). This terminological shift has important conceptual implications: while "assisting" denotes an ancillary action, which entails that the principal action is performed by the person who is assisted (in this case, the irregular immigrant), "procuring" denotes instead a stand-alone action, with a meaning of its own; this difference is confirmed by the fact that while the FD describes the role of the smuggled migrant by using verbs ("assisting someone to enter", "to transit", "to stay"), thus revealing that the person is seen as someone actively contributing to the whole deed, the UNPS, on the contrary, uses—at least in art. 3, letter a—a noun ("procuring the entry of someone"), thus describing the migrant's position more as the result of another person's action than as an action itself.

We can thus say that in the UNPS the smuggler's conduct is recognised to have wrongness of its own: wrongness that is not a mere reflection of irregular

---

85 On which see, extensively, Gallagher and David (n 48).

86 But see Pablo Rodríguez Ocotrinillo, 'Non-criminalization of smuggled migrants (Notes on the interpretation of article 5 of the Protocol against the Smuggling of Migrants by Land, Sea and Air) [2014] 2 (available at: www.acnur.org/t3/fileadmin/Documentos/BDL/2014/9791.pdf?view=1).

87 To be honest, this does not mean that the Protocol itself is not open to criticism (see, e.g. Anne T. Gallagher, 'Human Rights and the New UN Protocols on Trafficking and Migrant Smuggling: A Preliminary Analysis' [2001] Human Rights Quarterly 996 ff.). However, there is little doubt that its approach is far more attentive to smuggled migrants' rights than is the EU legislation.

migration, but derives directly from its being a commodification of human beings,[88] an exploitation of the migrant's vulnerability as a source of enrichment, of money-making. And indeed, as we have seen (above, § 1.6), according to the definition in art. 3, letter a, the "procurement of the illegal entry of a person" does not amount to smuggling unless it is committed "in order to obtain, directly or indirectly, a financial or other material benefit" (but see also art. 6, sub-sec. 1):[89] the smuggler's aim of getting some material benefit from his conduct is a definitional element of the crime, which heavily contributes to shaping its wrongness in terms of exploitation, while, on the other hand, excludes from the scope of the criminalisation "the activities of those who provided support to migrants for humanitarian reasons or on the basis of close family ties."[90]

Particularly telling, moreover, is art. 5 UNPS, according to which "Migrants shall not become liable to criminal prosecution under this Protocol for the fact of having been the object of" smuggling. This reinforces the idea that, in the UNPS's approach, the smuggled migrant is seen as the "object" of the smuggler's conduct, and not as an agent of the smuggling process. This is why being smuggled should never be blamed on him or her.[91]

Also interesting is the fact that, according to art. 6, sub-sec. 3, each state party should consider "as aggravating circumstances" the fact that the smuggling is performed in ways "(a) [t]hat endanger, or are likely to endanger, the lives or safety of the migrants concerned; or (b) [t]hat entail inhuman or degrading treatment, including for exploitation, of such migrants." The scope of this provision is far wider than that of the similar provision in art. 1, sub-sec. 3 of the FFD: while, as we have seen, the latter only gives relevance to migrants' lives being put at risk, the other goes as far as to give relevance to other aspects of the smuggled migrants' dignity and well-being.

1.8.3 *What Is/Are the Good/s Protected by Italian Law on Smuggling?*

It is now time to wonder what are the aims of Italian criminal law against migrant smuggling: is it principally aimed at protecting the state against irregular immigration, or is it principally aimed at protecting migrants against their smugglers? To put it differently, what position is thereby attributed to

---

88 *Legislative Guides for the Implementation of the UN Convention against Transnational Organized Crime and the Protocols thereto* (UNODC 2004, available at: https://www.unodc.org/pdf/crime/legislative_guides/Legislative%20guides_Full%20version.pdf) 349–350.

89 The "offences [of smuggling] should not apply to groups that smuggle migrants or asylum-seekers for reasons other than "financial or other material benefit"" (*Ibidem*).

90 United Nations—General Assembly (n 69) § 88 (but see also § 92).

91 See Rodríguez Ocotrinillo (n 86) 2.

smuggled migrants? Is Italian law against smuggling based on the EU complicity approach? Or is it based on the exploitation approach of the UNPS?

In general, I would say that the Italian approach to smuggling appears to be twofold: while criminalization of cross-border smuggling—particularly in the basic forms of sub-sec. 1—seems to be principally concerned with state interests, the criminalization of inland smuggling seems instead decidedly more attentive to the rights of the smuggled migrant.

As we have seen, Italian law, exactly like the FD, conceives the basic forms of cross-border smuggling independent of any possible harm to the smuggled foreigner. Inbound smuggling and outbound smuggling, in particular, are defined irrespective of the fact that smugglers pursue an aim of profit, thus irrespective of smugglers' action entailing any kind of harm or exploitation of those smuggled. It is true that the rights of the smuggled specifically enter the picture as soon as one takes into consideration the aggravated forms of cross-border smuggling in sub-secs. 3 and 3 ter (see above, § 1.7). Nonetheless, in these hypotheses, the protection of the smuggled is *in addition* to the criminal norm's fundamental aim, which remains that of protecting state interests. In its basic forms, cross-border smuggling does not entail any kind of necessary involvement of the foreigner's interests; these enter the picture only contingently and collaterally, expressing, so to speak, different and additional wrongness: they only become relevant by being *grafted* into a context to which, in principle, they do not belong.

This basic irrelevance of the needs of the smuggled persons within criminalization of their smuggling is further confirmed by the limited range of application attributed to the humanitarian defence by art. 12, sub-sec. 2: this means that—except for cases of absolute and extreme necessity—the humanitarian needs of foreigners heading for Italy are clearly given secondary importance compared to the interests of the state, at least when, as is the case with inbound smuggling, a violation of state borders is at stake.

In principle, Italian law does not consider the smuggled migrant to be a victim of cross-border smuggling:[92] he or she, along with the state, is only considered a victim of some of the aggravated forms of the crime; but in this case too he or she is not properly treated as a victim *of smuggling* (of which the state is considered the only victim), but as a victim either *of the concrete ways* in which the action is performed or *of the concrete aims* at which it is directed; his or her role as a victim is thus to be referred not to smuggling as such, but to further harmful dimensions which are contingent with respect to smuggling's basic wrongness.

92 Donini (n 58).

The smuggled foreigner is rather the material object of basic forms of cross-border smuggling:[93] the "thing" on which the smuggler's action is performed. This also emerges, quite clearly, from the terminology used to describe the criminal conduct, which echoes art. 3, letter a, UNPS: it is defined, as we already know, as the commission of acts aimed at illegally "procuring the entry of [the foreigner] into the territory of the state, or of a state of which the person is not a national or a permanent resident." We have already seen how both this language and this syntactic construction manifest a view of the smuggled foreigner as an object, whose position within the deed is not expressed by a verb, but by a noun, which seems to define it as the result of the action of other subjects. This is further confirmed by other expressions, which can be found in art. 12, referring to the smuggled migrant in an objectifying mood: in the first part of sub-secs. 1 and 3, he or she is depicted as the object of a "transport"; in letter b and c of sub-sec. 3, he or she is called, instead, as the "person carried"; in letter a of sub-sec. 3 ter, he or she is identified as a person "to employ" in illicit activities.

Art. 12, however, sharply departs from the UNPS approach as regards the requirement that conduct be performed for profit. More generally, if we look at the whole system—and thus take crimes of cross-border smuggling as pieces of a wider project—we easily find out that Italian law is decidedly oriented toward the complicity approach, and is fundamentally informed by the idea that the fundamental reason to criminalize (cross-border) smuggling lies in the need to protect the state against irregular immigration, or, better still, against the violation of its borders (thus, in the first place, against irregular immigrants themselves). Particularly telling, from this perspective, is the header of art. 12, that speaks of "Rules against clandestine immigrations", and thus clarifies from the outset what is the fundamental political concern underlying the criminalization of smuggling. In addition, from 2009 on, the very conduct of foreigners irregularly entering or staying in the territory of the state was made into a crime (art. 10 bis TUIMM). As a consequence, unless he or she was transported against his or her will (which would mean that different crimes were committed than smuggling, such as enslavement, trafficking or kidnapping), the foreigner smuggled toward Italy, simply in virtue of having been smuggled, himself or herself commits a crime. While his or her "formal" position in the structure of art. 12, sub-sec. 1, is that of a mere "object" of the smuggler's action, his or her "substantial" position, as results from the combined provisions of art. 12 and art. 10 bis, is that of an accomplice of the smuggler: rather, he or she appears to be the author of the principal wrong, that against which state criminalization

93 *Ibidem.*

is principally directed, that is "clandestine immigration." Foreigners disembarking on the Sicilian coasts crammed in unseaworthy dinghies, or caught hidden in the back of a car crossing the border between Slovenia and Italy, are regularly charged with the crime of "clandestine immigration": even in those cases—which are all too frequent—in which the transport has put at risk their lives or their physical integrity, or in which—during the journey—they have been subjected to inhuman and degrading treatment. In sum, they remain the authors of a crime (art. 10 bis) even in those cases in which their being smuggled entails a violation of their own rights.[94] This is due, as I have mentioned earlier, to the fact that the violation of these rights is not consubstantial with the crimes of cross-border smuggling, which in their basic wrongness revolve around the violation of state borders.

This does not hold, instead, for inland smuggling. From what has been said above with regard to the meaning of both the aim of profit requirement and the humanitarian defence in sub-sec. 2, the consequence can be drawn that both forms of this crime (the general form, in sub-sec. 5, and the special one, in sub-sec. 5 bis) necessarily entail an exploitation of the foreigner's irregular condition, which must be seen as exploitation of the foreigner himself or herself, made possible by the weakness of his or her position before the law. If this is correct, though it might be at odds with the general direction of Italian law on immigrants and immigration (a direction more concerned with protecting state borders against irregular crossings than with protecting foreigners against smuggling),[95] it must be said that the focus of crimes of inland smuggling is on the protection of the smuggled foreigner, at least in part and exactly because the definition of the crime revolves around the aim of exploitation of the foreigner's legal and social weakness; facilitation of the foreigner's irregular stay is thus only relevant as an aspiration to its exploitation by the smuggler. More precisely, the crime can be ascribed to the category of so-called multi-harmful crimes, since it criminalizes inland smuggling as harming both, and at the same time, the interest of the state in proper enforcement of its immigration rules and the interest of the foreigner—irregularly finding himself or herself in the territory of the state—that his or her condition of legal and social weakness is not made worse by persons trying to exploit it for profit.

---

94 Except, of course, in cases of *smuggling interruptus*, in which their conduct stops before arriving in the state's territorial sea and their entrance therein is not their conduct, but a consequence of their being rescued: in such cases, what they do is, structurally, merely attempting to irregularly enter the state's territory; the crime in art. 10 bis is a mere contravention, and attempted contraventions are not punishable according to Italian law. Cf. Cass., Sec. I, 30.1.2017, no. 14694.

95 Cf. Donini (n 58).

Ultimately, the Italian way of criminalizing migrant smuggling, considered as a whole, appears to be marked by a sort of schizophrenia: while in general it is clearly attuned to EU policies on migration, and thus characterized by adherence to the so-called "complicity approach" (which uses criminalization of smuggling as a way of indirectly criminalizing irregular trans-border movements), when it comes to inland smuggling it seems instead to be more attuned to the so-called "exploitation approach" typical of the UNPS, which it pushes forward to the point of considering the smuggled migrant not a mere "object", but the victim of a crime (defined as a crime of exploitation of the foreigner's weakness).

The figure of the migrant that emerges is thus manifold: if we only look at sub-secs. 1 and 3 of art. 12, he or she appears as the material object of the smuggler's activity; a soon as the focus is expanded so as also to take into account the link between art. 12 and art. 10 bis TUIMM, the image emerges of the foreigner as an "irregular migrant", he himself or she herself author of a crime substantially linked to that of the smuggler. Finally, when it comes to inland smuggling, the foreigner ceases to be either a mere object or an accomplice of the smuggler, becoming its victim, along with the state.

Bibliography

Ashworth, Andrew and Lucia Zedner, *Preventive Justice* (Oxford University Press 2014).

Allsopp, Jennifer, 'Contesting *fraternité*. Vulnerable migrants and the politics of protection in contemporary France' [2012] RSC Working Paper Series (available at: https://www.rsc.ox.ac.uk/files/files-1/wp82-contesting-fraternite-2012.pdf).

Allsopp, Jennifer, 'The European Facilitation Directive and the Criminalisation of Humanitarian Assistance to Irregular Migrants: Measuring the Impact on the Whole Community', in Sergio Carrera, Elspeth Guild (eds.), *Irregular migration, trafficking and smuggling of human beings. Policy dilemmas in the EU* (CEPS 2016).

Basaran, Tugba, 'The saved and the drowned: Governing indifference in the name of security' [2016] Security Dialogue 205.

Bellagamba, Gianni and Giuseppe Cariti, *La nuova disciplina dell'immigrazione* (Giuffrè 2008).

Bellezza, Sara and Tiziana Calandrino, *Criminalization of Flight and Escape Aid* (borderline-europe 2017, available at: https://www.borderline-europe.de/sites/default/files/readingtips/Kidem%20final%20report%2005_2017.pdf).

Bhabha, Jacqueline and Monette Zard 'Smuggled or Trafficked?' [2006] Forced Migration Review 6.

Caputo, Angelo, *Diritto e procedura penale dell'immigrazione* (Giappichelli 2006).

Caputo, Angelo, 'I delitti di favoreggiamento delle migrazioni illegali', in Id. and Giorgio Fidelbo, *Reati in materia di immigrazione e di stupefacenti* (Giappichelli 2012).

Cuttitta, Paolo 'Repoliticization Through Search and Rescue? Humanitarian NGOs and Migration Management in the Central Mediterranean' [2017] Geopolitics DOI: 10.1080/14650045.2017.1344834 (available at: https://www.tandfonline.com/doi/full/10.1080/14650045.2017.1344834).

De Bruycker, Philippe, Anna Di Bartolomeo and Philippe Fargues, 'Migrant smuggled by sea to the EU: Facts, laws and policy options' [2013] MPC Research Report 4 (available at: http://www.migrationpolicycentre.eu/docs/MPC-RR-2013-009.pdf).

Donini, Massimo, 'Il cittadino extracomunitario da *oggetto materiale* a *tipo d'autore* nel controllo penale dell'immigrazione' [2009] Questione giustizia 101.

European Commission, 'EU Action Plan against Migrant Smuggling (2015–2020)', COM(2015) 285 final, Brussels, 27.05.2015Europol, 'Migrant Smuggling in the EU', Feb. 2016 (available at: https://www.europol.europa.eu/publications-documents/migrant-smuggling-in-eu).

Guild, Elspeth and Sergio Carrera (2013), 'EU Borders and Their Controls. Preventing unwanted movement of people in Europe?' [2013] CEPS Essay (available at: https://www.ceps.eu/system/files/No%206%20EU%20Borders%20and%20their%20Controls%20revised.pdf).

Gallagher, Anne T., 'Human Rights and the New UN Protocols on Trafficking and Migrant Smuggling: A Preliminary Analysis' [2001] Human Rights Quarterly 996.

Gallagher, Anne T. and Fiona David, *The International Law of Migrant Smuggling* (Cambridge University Press 2014).

Horder, Jeremy, 'Harmless Wrongdoing and the Anticipatory Perspective on Criminalization', in G.R. Sullivan and Ian H. Dennis (eds.), *Seeking Security: Pre-Empting the Commission of Criminal Harms* (Hart Publishing 2012) 79.

Johannes, Hartmut, *Mittelbare Täterschaft bei rechtmäßigem Handeln des Werkzeuges* (Klostermann 1963).

Landry, Rachel, 'Decriminalising 'Humanitarian Smuggling' [2017] RSC Research in Brief (available at https://www.rsc.ox.ac.uk/publications/research-in-brief-decriminalising-humanitarian-smuggling/@@download/file).

Legislative Guides for the Implementation of the UN Convention against Transnational Organized Crime and the Protocols thereto (UNODC 2004, available at: https://www.unodc.org/pdf/crime/legislative_guides/Legislative%20guides_Full%20version.pdf).

Masera, Luca, 'Immigrazione', in Oliviero Mazza and Francesco Viganò (eds.), *Misure urgenti in materia di sicurezza pubblica* (Giappichelli 2008).

Mitsilegas, Valsamis, *The Criminalization of Migration in Europe. Challenges for Human Rights and the Rule of Law* (Springer 2015).

Model Law against the Smuggling of Migrants (UNODC 2010, available at: https://www.unodc.org/documents/human-trafficking/Model_Law_Smuggling_of_Migrants_10-52715_Ebook.pdf).

Obokata, Tom, 'Smuggling of Human Beings from a Human Rights Perspective: Obligations of Non-State and State Actors under International Human Rights Law' [2005] International Journal of Refugee Law 394.

Ocotrinillo, Pablo Rodríguez, 'Non-criminalization of smuggled migrants (Notes on the interpretation of article 5 of the Protocol against the Smuggling of Migrants by Land, Sea and Air) [2014] (available at: www.acnur.org/t3/fileadmin/Documentos/BDL/2014/9791.pdf?view=1).

Roxin, Claus, *Täterschaft und Tatherrschaft* (7th edn., Walter de Gruyter & Co. 1999).

Spena, Alessandro, 'Human smuggling and irregular immigration in the EU: from complicity to exploitation?', in Sergio Carrera, Elspeth Guild (eds.), *Irregular migration, trafficking and smuggling of human beings. Policy dilemmas in the EU* (CEPS 2016) 33.

Smuggled Futures: The dangerous path of a migrant from Africa to Europe, Geneva: Global Initiative against Transnational Organised Crime (Global Initiative against Transnational Organised Crime 2014, available at: www.globalinitiative.net/smuggled-futures/).

Smuggling of migrants into, through and from North Africa (UNODC 2010, available at: www.unodc.org/documents/human-trafficking/Migrant_smuggling_in_North_Africa_June_2010_ebook_E_09-87293.pdf).

Spieker, Heike, 'The Right to Give and Receive Humanitarian Assistance', in Hans-Joachim Heintze, Andrej Zwitter (eds.), *International Law and Humanitarian Assistance. A Crosscut Through Legal Issues Pertaining to Humanitarianism* (Springer 2011) 7.

Triandafillidou, Anna, *Migrant Smuggling. Irregular Migration from Asia and Africa to Europe* (Palgrave MacMillan 2012).

United Nations—General Assembly, 'Interpretive notes for the official records (travaux préparatoires) of the negotiation of the United Nations Conventions against Transnational Organized Crime and the Protocols thereto' [2000] A/55/383/Add. 1.

Ventrella, Matilde, 'Recognizing Effective Legal Protection to People Smuggled at Sea, by Reviewing the EU Legal Framework on Human Trafficking and Solidarity between Member States' [2015] Social Inclusion 76.

Ventrella, Matilde, *The Control of People Smuggling and Trafficking in the EU: Experiences from the UK and Italy* (Routledge 2016).

Part 2. Trafficking in Human Beings vs. Migrant Smuggling: a Dangerous Relationship

Vincenzo Militello

2.1 The Double Track of Human Trafficking: an Introduction*

On an initial consideration, human trafficking appears to be among the most emblematic forms of contemporary criminality. In its conventional instances, it consists of a profit-driven[1] and gender-based[2] transnational organized crime.[3]

To perform a thorough analysis of the phenomenon, its hidden features[4] must be taken into consideration. Its perpetrators frequently remain unpunished;[5]

---

* Some of the arguments in this contribution have been already presented in previous seminars and conferences: "I diritti e le frontiere" (*Palace of Justice*, Agrigento, 25–26 September 2015); "Criminalidad organizada transnacional" (*University of Salamanca*, 5–6 November 2016); International Conference "18 de Outubro—Dia Europeu contra o Tráfico de Seres Humanos" (*Facultade de Direito da Universidade de Coimbra*, 18–19 October 2017). Many thanks to Elena Militello for the English translation.

1 On the *business* of human trafficking see John Salt and Jeremy Stein, 'Migration as a Business: the case of Trafficking' [1997] Intern. migration 467 f.; Louise Shelley, *Human Trafficking. A Global Perspective* (Cambridge University Press 2010) 112 f.

2 In the forms of sexual exploitation, which remain the most widespread (from 2007 to 2014 they were between 53 and 59% of all the cases discovered, according to *Global Report on Trafficking in Persons 2016* (UNODC, 2017) 6, available at https://www.unodc.org/documents/data-and-analysis/glotip/2016_Global_Report_on_Trafficking_in_Persons.pdf), the female victims are absolutely prevalent. See also *e.g.* Stephanie Hepburn and Luise Simon, *Human Trafficking Around the World* (Columbia University Press 2013) 2; Sanja Ćopić and Biljana Simeunović-Patić, 'Victims of Human Trafficking. Meeting Victim/s Needs?', in John Winterdyk, Benjamin Perrin and Philip Reichel (eds.), *Human trafficking. Exploring the International Nature, Concerns and Complexities* (CRC Press 2012) 268.

3 Neil Boister, *An Introduction to Transnational Criminal Law* (Oxford University Press) 39 f.; Shelley (n 1) 2, 5 f., 83 f.; Sally Stoecker and Louise Shelley (eds.), *Human Trafficking and Transnational Crime: Eurasian and American perspectives* (Rowman & Littlefield 2005); Costanza Bernasconi, 'La repressione penale della tratta di esseri umani nell'ordinamento italiano, in Serena Forlati (ed.), *La lotta alla tratta di esseri umani fra dimensione internazionale e ordinamento interno* (Jovene 2013) 70 f.

4 Scott Decker, 'Human Trafficking: context and connections to conventional crime' [2015] *Journal of Crime and Justice* 291.

5 Anne Gallagher, *The International Law of Human Trafficking* (Cambridge University Press 2010) 370 f.

its victims are often "invisible", coerced by traffickers.[6] All said elements are relevant to the countering actions. It is troublesome to define the phenomenon in its essential traits, to distinguish it from other kinds of illicit conducts and to frame its specific features and the meaningful connections to other socio-economical events, above all migrations and international mobility of persons characterizing globalization.[7]

The focus of the present article is the latter point of view and its legal consequences, as they highlight the difficult relationship between the actual events involved and their translation into formal norms. This affects national case law, which remains unsettled on the unruly matter of the border line between trafficking and illegal migrations.

Indeed, the issue covers a much wider range of perspectives than the legal one now under scrutiny. It can affect the determination of international routes for trafficking;[8] it can be even harder to define when the criminal conducts are carried out within one single state; it cannot easily be either measured how common and widespread the phenomenon is, at the global, regional (*i.e.* in a group of states)[9] or merely national[10] level; or estimated what amounts of money or value it may involve. At the same time, there are complex issues of criminal policy at the heart of the fight against such a multi-faceted phenomenon and there are delicate questions of interpretation linked to the manner in which different legal systems deal with it.

---

6 Susan Kneebone and Julie Debeljak, *Transnational crime and Human Rights. Responses to Human Trafficking in the Greater Mekong Region* (Routledge 2012) 10.

7 On the problem of the relation with the migrant smuggling see e.g. Salt and Stein (n 1) 469 f.; Jackie Turner and Liz Kelly, 'Trade Secrets: Intersections between Diasporas and Crime Groups in the Constitution of the Human Trafficking Chain' [2009] *British Journal of Criminology* 184 f.; Maggy Lee, *Trafficking and Global Crime Control* (Sage 2011) 85 f.

8 For a comparison with drug-trafficking, see Decker (nt. 4) 292.

9 For various examples, see Stef Janssens, 'Fenomeenanalyse van mensenhandel' in Charles-Éric Clesse (ed.) *Traite des être humains Mensenhandel—Mensenmokkel* (Die Keure, 2010), 39; Johan Leman and Stef Janssens, *Human Trafficking and Migrant Smuggling in Southeast Europe and Russia. Learning Criminal Entrepreneurship and Traditional Culture* (Palgrave Macmillan 2015); Sallie Yea (ed.), *Human Trafficking in Asia. Forcing issues* (Routledge 2015).

10 On the difficulty of measuring the phenomenon, despite the plurality of sources on the subject (*International Organization for Migration; Human Rights Watch*; U.N. Office on Drugs and Crime—UNODOC, *International Labour Office*), see HEPBURN/SIMON (n 2), 5. See also Karolis Zibas, 'Exploitative Sham Marriages and Trafficking in Human Beings in Lithuania', in Minna Viuhko and others (eds.), *Exploitative Sham Marriages: Exploring the Links between Human Trafficking and Sham Marriages in Estonia, Ireland, Latvia, Lithuania and Slovakia* (HEUNI 2016) 254 (available at http://www.heuni.fi/material/attachments/heuni/reports/ci5Y5cgbB/Nettiin.pdf).

Since it would not be possible to cover all the different issues, in the present enquiry the focus will be on the normative response to human trafficking, from the different possible approaches to the subject (§ 2.2), to their description at the different supranational levels in order to fight and prevent this crime (§§ 2.3–4). In particular, it will assess how the normative response impacts on the position of victims, in light of the difference between trafficking and smuggling enshrined in international legal texts (§§ 2.5–6). It will then discuss how they have been implemented in the Italian legal system, using national case law as a case study to prove the importance of a proper understanding of the relationship between human trafficking and illegal migrations (§ 2.7).

As a starting point, it will be noted that a common core of trafficking can be outlined, where older and newer features coexist, regardless of the already mentioned variety of the current manifestations. This common core consists in creating or facilitating, through means of interposition often with very modern traits (international travels, Internet contacts ...), ancient conditions of exploitation, *e.g.* sexual or work exploitation, where the human being is used as a tool by another subject to obtain some kind of gain.

The fact that trafficking is based on an interpersonal relationship of this nature explains why it is often referred to as a "modern form of slavery", by the public,[11] in the laws,[12] in case law,[13] and even before that in theoretical discussions.[14]

The general abolition of the condition of slavery as a legal status for human beings does not per se forbid us to think of the relevant situation in human trafficking as analogical to slavery, at least from the point of view of criminal law, which is concerned with substantial protection of the underlying values.

11 As important examples see the introduction of the U.S. Secretary of State, *J. Kerry*, to the U.S. Department of State, 'Trafficking in person report 2015', 2 f. (available at https://2009-2017.state.gov/documents/organization/245365.pdf); the Joint Declaration of Religious Leaders Against Modern Slavery, signed on December, 2 2014 in Vatican City (available at https://www.globalfreedomnetwork.org/declaration); the declaration of the European Commissioner for Home Affairs *C. Malmström* of 18 October 2012 in Christoph Lindner, *Die Effektivität transnationaler Maßnahmen gegen Menschenhandel in Europa* (Mohr Siebeck 2014) 1.

12 See in the U.K. the *Modern Slavery Act 2015*.

13 For example, in the famous case *Rantsev* (European Court of Human Rights, *Rantsev v. Cyprus and Russia*, n. 25965/04, of 7.1.2010, par. 281).

14 Since Kevin Bales, *Disposable people. New Slavery in the Global Economy* (1999) it. ed. *I nuovi schiavi. La merce umana nell'economia globale* (Feltrinelli 2004). See also Silvia Scarpa, *Trafficking in Human Beings. Modern Slavery* (Oxford University Press 2008); Maria Cristina Barbieri, 'La riduzione in schiavitù: un passato che non vuole passare. Un'indagine storica sulla costruzione e i limiti del tipo' [2010] Materiali per una storia della cultura giuridica 283 f.; Paola Scevi, *Nuove schiavitù e diritto penale* (Giuffrè 2014).

There is an affinity of living conditions that does not need to become a status of total subjugation of the area of free actions of the person, as was quintessential to the traditional forms of slavery. It would be sufficient that only one of the forms in which the personality of the victim may be expressed is limited to the point of identifying a relationship of full submission to another person. These are the conditions that can be found in the different activities that constitute the purpose of trafficking: sexual exploitation, illegal labour, mendicancy, and transplants of human organs. There are also more specific purposes that involve further offences: sexual exploitation of minors, child mendicancy, and conscription of child soldiers. Or, in addition, there are activities that can be linked to those already listed, like forced marriages[15] or illegal adoptions.

In all of these cases, it does not matter what is the underlying legal interest ("*bene giuridico*") specifically protected by the norms defining the offence. One can always perceive in the background the dignity of the person, being disrespected in its minimal conditions of free exercise of the discretion to choose the course of one's action given to any human being.

2.2 The Different Approaches toward Countering Trafficking: Human Rights vs. Security and the Need for Integration

Making reference to human dignity in the context of human trafficking points to a specific approach to the counteractions considering the human rights of victims and aimed at ensuring the highest possible protection for them, even with forms of assistance and support.[16]

Human dignity is indeed a meta-value among human rights and its path of progressive acknowledgement by the international community marked the increasing awareness that there is a need to counter human trafficking.

The antinomy between the relevant values at stake is patent in the most recent step in the path of human rights, that is the EU Charter of fundamental

15 Viuhko and others (n 10).

16 For a *human-rights-based approach* to human trafficking see *e.g.* Julia Planitzer, *Trafficking in Human Beings and Human Rights* (Neuer Wissenschaftlicher Verlag 2014) 21 ff., 89 f.; Connie Rijken, 'A Human Rights Based Approach to Trafficking in Human Beings' [2009] Security and Human Rights 212 f.; Tom Obokata, *Trafficking in Human Beings from a Human Rights Perspective: Towards a more Holistic Approach* (Martinus Nijhoff Publishers 2006) 121 f.

rights. It commences by stressing the inviolability of human dignity in Art. 1 and then explicitly prohibits trafficking in human beings in Art. 5.[17]

The issue is also considered in a pivotal text for the history of the international protection of human rights: the Statute of the International Criminal Court. It lists among international crimes, in its part dedicated to substantive criminal law, "trafficking in persons, in particular women and children" as a form of the crime against humanity of "enslavement", if committed in a specific context, "as part of a widespread or systematic attack directed against any civilian population, with knowledge of the attack" (art. 7, sub-sec. 1, letter c and sub-sec. 2, letter c).[18]

This link is now also prevalent in the context of protection of human rights enforced by the European Court of Human Rights (ECtHR). It ruled that trafficking in human beings is in contrast with the rationale behind the prohibition of slavery and forced labour enshrined in art. 4 of the European Convention on Human Rights (ECHR).[19] It highlighted the instrumental use made of the victims of trafficking by the traffickers, who treat them like goods on which to exercise typical ownership powers.

The different concurring references to the protection of fundamental rights show that, considering the relevant values in the field, it would not be appropriate to deal with the countering of trafficking within a single national legal system. That is also true because of the transnational nature of various contemporary forms of trafficking and their connections with the general issue of globalization and its effects on the mobility of humans. It is the subject-matter with its distinctive features that triggered a transnational intervention, here as in other fields where the need for harmonization of criminal systems was more and more felt in the last decades.

This observation is not sufficient to solve the key issue of the approach to this phenomenon by different levels of intervention. There is a different attitude to human rights threatened by the conducts of trafficking and it focuses on the safety of society.

Unlike the former perspective, which revolves around the position of the victim, the latter aims at countering illicit conducts efficiently, threatening their authors with criminal sanctions, to be imposed proportionally to the

17 Sophie Tschorr, *Trafficking of human beings* (Oldenburger Verlag für Wirtschaft, Informatik und Recht 2015) 27 f.

18 Obokata (n 16) 133 f.

19 ECtHR, *Rantsev* (n 13); see also *Siliadin v. France*, 26 Juli 2005 (n. 73316/01). On these cases, for example, David Mancini, 'Il cammino europeo nel contrasto alla tratta di persone' [2010, n 9] Diritto Penale e Processo 7 f.; Scevi (n 14) 15 f.

seriousness of the offence.[20] To execute this kind of conducts there must be a complex organizational lay-out, for an extended period of time and generally carried out by an organized group of subjects that may be located in different countries. Such criminal organizations pose threats to the state and society, both because they develop a criminal system involving other violent crimes around trafficking and because they earn huge profits out of it, which may later be used to buy weapons or drugs and/or to finance terrorism-related activities.[21]

The safety approach can be implemented through different criminal policies: from a traditional one, which counters these activities through criminal sanctions, to a more recent one, whose main feature is an economic approach, treating trafficking as an illegal business.[22] The latter policy places the features of trafficking within the more general context of illegal markets: it has emerged that it is the third largest among them, after drugs and weapons. These estimates should only be taken into account as a general indication, since it is extremely difficult to collect reliable data.[23] Economic analysis of criminal issues impacts intervention strategies: it favours financial sanctions on revenues from illicit conducts, more than detention sanctions against the authors of the crimes. This is in line with the widespread tendency to target illicit financial assets derived from activities of criminal organizations.

Despite the fact that these different approaches are sometimes presented as conflicting,[24] the preferred path to efficient countering of the phenomenon should include and evaluate the different contribution that each of them can make.[25] On the one hand, prosecuting illicit trafficking activities is a prerequisite to ensure the dignity of the victims, as well as their fundamental rights. On the other hand, without forms of protection of and assistance to the victims it

---

20 Anna Jonsson, 'Introduction' in Ead. (ed.), *Human Security and Human Trafficking* (Routeledge 2009) 1 f.

21 See *e.g.* Louise Shelley, 'Human Security and Human Trafficking', in Jonsson (ed.) (n 20), 10 f.

22 Arumendra K. Pandey, 'Economic Rehabilitation: A human approach to combat human trafficking', in Veerendra Mishra (ed.), *Human Trafficking. The stakeholders' perspective* (Sage 2013), 340; Jennifer Suchland, *Economies of violence. Transnational feminism, Postsocialism and the Politics of Sex Trafficking* (Duke University Press, 2015).

23 Tschorr (n 17), 12; Lindner (n 11), 1.

24 See Claudia Aradau, 'The Perverse Politics of Four-Letter Word: Risk and Pity in the Securitisation of Human Trafficking' [2004] *Millenium: Journal of international Studies* 251 f.; Sarah Krieg, 'Trafficking in human beings: The EU approach between border control, law enforcement and human rights' [2009] European Law Journal 776 f.; Marie Segrave, *Human Trafficking* (Ashgate 2013) XVII; Lee (n 7) 83 f.

25 See Karin Bruckmüller and Stepan Schumann, 'Crime control versus Social Work Approaches in the Context of the "3P" Paradigm', in Winterdyk, Perrin and Reichel (eds.) (n 2), 104 f.; Krieg (n 24) 785.

is not easy to break the circle of fear isolating the individual victim of trafficking and to allow his or her collaboration with the justice system.

The economic perspective is also useful, not only to come up with the most efficient methods of countering illicit revenues from trafficking, but also to allow the connection between it and other illicit markets based on the exchange of different goods (weapons, drugs, tobacco, vital organs, and also counterfeited prescription drugs or cultural heritage).[26] From this point of view, too, it can be confirmed that human trafficking uses victims as material goods, perceived in their potential for economic exploitation, contrary to their most basic human dignity.

The different approaches to countering trafficking must therefore be considered combined and convergent, to implement an intervention strategy that are solidly grounded in values and at the same time take advantage of the expertise and working practices of each point of view.[27]

Recalling the protection of human dignity is useful to settle potential contrasts arising from such integration: since dignity is a meta-value, above all others, it cannot be neglected even when the immediate aims of public actions are more specific and limited.[28]

First, the efficacy of the chosen measures should be analysed, so that the coercive interventions of crime control can be coordinated with adequate forms of assistance to the victims to prevent "unintentional and undesirable secondary effects that persecution policies might cause by increasing the vulnerabilities of trafficking."[29] At the same time, the overarching value of human dignity should be acknowledged: this will make it possible to interpret differently human trafficking and the more general issues surrounding it. It will also prevent excessive parcelling into detailed different analyses (which are undeniably useful to face specific issues) from hiding the bigger picture of the phenomenon.[30]

26 Tschorr (n 17) 13.
27 Mishra, 'Introduction', in Id. (ed.) (n 22) 4 f.
28 This role of human dignity as support to other more specific values is not always adequately considered: for example by Liane Wörner, 'Penal theory and the protection of life—the human dignity argument and its inconsistencies in German criminal law', in Arndt Sinn (Hg.), *Menschenrechte und Strafrecht*, (V&R unipress 2013), 25 f., 33 f.
29 *Report of the Experts Group on Trafficking in Human Beings* (Brussels, 2004) available at https://ec.europa.eu/anti-trafficking/eu-policy/report-experts-group-trafficking-human-beings_en. This group was set up by the European Commission (Decision 2003/209/CE of 25 March 2003. On the risk of secondary victimization see also Bruckmüller and Schumann (n 25) 105.
30 Gallagher (n 5) 3. See also again Bruckmüller and Schumann (n 25) 104.

2.3 A New Integrated Perspective on International Counter-action

At the supranational level, such a holistic approach to the fight against trafficking has taken hold, one that focuses not only on coercion but also on the rights of the victims.

EU Directive 2011/36/EU is the most recent step in the path toward the formalization of internationals duties of protection in this matter: it expressly displays the fundamental choice favouring this approach (Recital 7); it recalls norms protecting victims, and also the aim of prevention, beyond the criminal system alone and calling for collaboration with civil society (Recital 7); at the same time, it recognizes criminal coercion, also in the forms of seizure and confiscation as described in the relevant international sources (Recital 13).

Similarly, and shortly afterwards, the EU Commission issued its Strategy towards the Eradication of Trafficking in Human Beings for the timeframe 2012–2016.[31] There, five key priorities reflecting the blossoming of that integrated approach are identified: identifying and protecting victims; prevention; persecution; cooperation among key actors, public and private; increased knowledge of distinctive features.

Increasing complexity in public policies countering trafficking is a common trait of all supranational sources dealing at various levels with the counteraction and progressively identifying which traits thereof might be legally significant. The most important of these sources, for its global nature, the wide range of its contents, and its impact on subsequent legal actions, not only at the national level,[32] is the Trafficking in Persons Protocol (UNPT) to the UN Convention against Transnational Organised Crime (so-called Palermo Convention).[33]

---

31 Communication from the Commission to the EU-Parlament and other of 19 June 2012 COM(2012) 286 fin, 'EU Strategy towards the Eradication of Trafficking in Human Beings 2012–2016'.

32 The main legally binding global instrument to fight human trafficking, as considered *e.g.* by Gallagher (n 5) 68.

33 The U.N. Convention against Transnational organized Crime and the related Protocols on *Trafficking in Persons* and *Smuggling of Migrants* were adopted by the General Assembly on 15 November 2000, open to the signature of Member States in the Palermo Conference of 12–15 December 2000, entered internationally into force respectively on 29 September 2003, 25 December 2003 and 28 January 2004. Together with a third Protocol on Firearms (adopted by the General Assembly on March 31, 2001 and in force since July 3, 2005), they were ratified by Italy with law 146 of 16 March 2006. On the latter, see Alberto Di Martino, 'Criminalità organizzata e reato transnazionale, diritto penale nazionale: l'attuazione in Italia della c.d. Convenzione di Palermo' [2007 n.1] Diritto penale e processo 15 s.

On the Palermo Convention see Hans Jorg Albrecht and Cyrille Fijnaut (eds.) *The Containment of Transnational Organized Crime. Comments of the UN Convention of December 2000*, (Iuscrim, 2002); Dimitri Vlassis, 'The UN Convention against

This specific protocol is devoted to prevention, suppression and punishment of trafficking in persons, especially women and children. Among its purposes there are also protection of and assistance to the victims (art. 6), and cooperation among the state parties (art. 2). It also provides a formal definition of trafficking, which is important to harmonize how national systems criminalise the relevant conducts (arts. 3 and 5).[34] The definition of trafficking emerges from a century-long history and it has a forerunner in the norms introduced by the international community to counter slavery.[35] It is built on three elements: types of relevant conducts, methods used, and purposes. The resulting offence is sufficiently precise: it encompasses more conducts than many of the subsequent national norms do. As an example, the important *US Trafficking Victims Protection Act* does not include non-sexual forms of exploitation.[36] Nevertheless, in more recent supranational interventions there are further

---

Transnational Organized Crime', in Mats Berdal and Monica Serrano (eds.), *Transnational Organized Crime and International Security: Business as Usual* (Lyenne Renner 2002), 83 f.; Vincenzo Militello, 'Le strategie di contrasto della criminalità organizzata transnazionale tra esigenze di politica criminale e tutela dei diritti umani', in Carola Parano and Alessandro Centonze (cur.), *L'attività di contrasto alla criminalità organizzata. Lo stato dell'arte* (Giuffrè 2005) 243 f.; John D. MCCLEAN, *Transnational Organized Crime. A commentary on the UN Convention and its Protocols* (Oxford University Press 2007); Gualtiero Michelini and Gioacchino Polimeni, 'Il fenomeno del crimine transnazionale e la convenzione delle NU contro il crimine organizzato transnazionale', in Elisabetta Rosi (ed.), *Criminalità organizzata transnazionale e sistema penale italiano* (IPSOA, 2007), 3 f.; Alessandro Centonze, *Criminalità organizzata e reati transnazionali* (Milano 2008), 117 f.; Laura Zúñiga Rodriguez, *Criminalidad organizada y sistema de derecho penal* (Comares 2009), 48 f.; Gianluca Ponti, *Crimini transnazionali e diritto internazionale* (Giuffrè, 2010); Almir Maljević, *'Participation in a Criminal Organisation' and 'Conspiracy'* (Duncker & Humblot 2011); Patricia Faraldo Cabana, *Asociaciones ilícitas y organizaciones criminales en el código penal español* (Tirant lo Blanc 2012), 37 f.; Anne Gallagher and Fiona David, *The International Law of Migrant Smuggling* (Cambridge University Press 2010), 34 f.

34 Pursuant to art. 3 UNPT: "*Trafficking in persons shall mean the recruitment, transportation, transfer, harbouring or receipt of persons, by means of the threat or use of force or other forms of coercion, of abduction, of fraud, of deception, of the abuse of power or of a position of vulnerability or of the giving or receiving of payments or benefits to achieve the consent of a person having control over another person, for the purpose of exploitation. Exploitation shall include, at a minimum, the exploitation of the prostitution of others or other forms of sexual exploitation, forced labour or services, slavery or practices similar to slavery, servitude or the removal of organs.*"

35 See Gallagher (n. 5), 13 f.

36 Critically on this point *e.g.* Alison Brysk and Austin Choi-Fitzpatrick, 'Rethinking Trafficking', in Id. and Id. (eds.), *From Human Trafficking to Human Rights: Reframing Contemporary Slavery* (University of Pennsylvania 2012) 2. Indeed, for a positive judgement on the Protocol, e.g. Maria Grazia Giammarinaro, Il protocollo sulla tratta degli esseri umani, in Rosi (ed.), (n 33), 420 f.

specifications of the standard: *e.g.* the 2002 EU Framework Decision on trafficking[37] mirrors the offence definition of the Palermo Protocol but it also specifies the levels of sanctions for each conduct (art. 3).

All in all, the Protocol outlines the foundations of counteraction of trafficking, which lie in prevention, victim protection, persecution, and also international cooperation.[38]

2.4 Prevention as a Criminal Policy Tendency inside the UN Protocol

In the provisions of the Protocol, a diversity of approach between the persecution part and the prevention part is undeniable. In the first of these parts, criminalizing relevant conducts is structured as an internationally binding obligation (art. 5); the second one is instead more flexible, giving more leeway to national choices in ensuring assistance to victims and preventing trafficking, although it describes a detailed framework of possible actions.[39] This diversity is at times overemphasized as if there was a rupture between the two different approaches within the Protocol. Accordingly, the criminal prosecution reaction would be preferred, while protection of the human rights of trafficking victims would be neglected or just left "in a quagmire", only referred to as an "addition", whose provisions are only "planned or ambitious."[40]

In this regard, it is to be noted that not every provision in the field of prevention and victim assistance is non-binding: art. 6 of the Protocol states that each State Party *shall* endeavour to provide for the physical safety of victims and shall *ensure* that there be a possibility of obtaining compensation for the damage suffered (sub-sec. 5 and 6); pursuant to art. 9, States Parties *shall* establish programmes both to prevent and combat trafficking and to protect victims

37 Council Framework Decision 2002/629/JHA of 19 July 2002 on combating trafficking in human beings OJ L203/1 of 1 August 2002).

38 For the "3P" paradigma (*Prevention, Protection, Persecution*, sometimes extended to the *Cooperation* o *Partnership* (in such case "3P plus C" o "4P") see *e.g.* Bruckmüller/Schumann (n 25), 105. For some critical factors on the implementation of such multilevel strategy Francesco Parisi, 'Il contrasto al traffico di esseri umani fra modelli normativi e risultati applicativi' [2016] Rivista italiana di diritto e procedura penale 1763 f.

39 See LEE (n 7), 83; David Nilken, 'Human Trafficking and Legal Culture' [2010] Israel law review 481.

40 See respectively James Hathaway 'The Human Rights Quagmire of "Human Trafficking"' [2008] Virginia Journal of International Law 30 f.; Kneebone and Debeljak (n 6), 11, 212 f.; Janie Chuang, 'Beyond a Snapshot: Preventing Human Trafficking in the Global Economy' [2006] Indiana Journal of Global Legal Studies 136 f., 148. See also Alessandra Annoni 'Gli obblighi internazionali in materia di tratta degli esseri umani', in Forlati (ed.) (n 3), 12.

from re-victimization (sub-sec. 1, letters A and B), as well as to alleviate the factors that make persons vulnerable to trafficking (sub-sec. 4) and to discourage the demand that fosters all forms of exploitation that lead to trafficking (sub-sec. 5).[41]

At the same time, this attitude toward prevention is not exclusive to the Protocol on Trafficking in Persons: a similar wording can be found in the Palermo Convention against Transnational Organised Crime. There, art. 31 mandates that States Parties shall *endeavour* to develop prevention policies against transnational organized crime (sub-sec. 1) and to reduce opportunities for organized criminal groups to launder the proceeds of crime (sub-sec. 2). An analogous pattern can also be found in the UN Merida Convention against Corruption. There, the part on preventing the phenomenon is dealt with in a complex set of provision (arts. 5–14), preceding the part on criminalisation and enforcement; nevertheless, it contains not only specific commitments (*e.g.* the creation of a specific agency to prevent corruption in art. 6) but also some provisions whose wording has a programmatic value, like those mentioned above (*e.g.* art. 5, sub-sec. 2, states that "each State Party *shall* endeavour to establish and promote effective practices aimed at the prevention of corruption" [emphasis added]).

This is therefore a critical issue that does not impact only the Protocol on Trafficking in Persons. It is unfortunately a generalized concern among supranational legal texts in the field of counteraction of forms of transnational crime. These supranational interventions are indeed predominantly aimed at drafting provisions to trigger prevention policies implemented by Member States. In these fields of intervention, the exchange of best practices and local partnerships are preferred. It is instead rare for the supranational sources to mandate binding standards to ensure prevention conditions, at least the basic ones, that are shared by all different states.

2.5 The Victims' Stance and the Difference between Trafficking and Smuggling

The recognition granted to victims in the trafficking protocol is one of its distinctive traits, as opposed to the other protocol to the same Palermo convention, on the smuggling of migrants. The latter protocol is aimed at preventing

41 On this point see the critic of Gallagher (n 5), 68.

and combating illegal smuggling of migrants, as well as at enhancing international cooperation between the Member States.[42]

There is no explicit mention of protection of victims' rights in the protocol, aimed at tackling those who favour illegal immigration. This does not arise out of absent-mindedness or an unfinished debate during preparatory works. During the negotiations of the Smuggling Protocol, several attempts were made to draw attention to the importance of migrants' rights. The result was that, as compared to the initial project, there are references to their protection in the final text, both in the Preamble ("*need to provide migrants with humane treatment and full protection of their rights*") and in some of the provisions (arts. 2, 4, 14, sub-sec. 2, expressly mentioning the rights of migrants, and art. 16 on "*protection and assistance measures*"). Nevertheless, the crucial point is that trafficked migrants are not acknowledged to be victims.[43]

The difference is directly linked to the fundamental boundary drawn by the international approach to legal construction of the two phenomena: trafficking always implies a person being subjected to another, who exploits them in the most various forms, all degrading the fundamental core of human dignity; smuggling is focused on states' interest to independently regulate access to their territory. In this case, the conduct is illicit because it damages a protected collective legal interest, not an individual one. As such, it is difficult to relate it to traditional forms of victims' protection, as they are mainly tailored to individual positions.

Still, even in this case, at the centre of the conduct to be countered there is always a real person, often among a multitude of other persons in the same position. In the reasoning of those legal texts which follow the lead of the UN Protocols, these persons are needed as elements for the execution of a prohibited conduct, while they stay out of the focus of the criminal offence. With regard to the peculiar legal position of the illegal migrant, Italian researchers have referred to them as "merely material objects" of the offence of smuggling.[44]

---

42 Art. 3 UNPS "a) *Smuggling of migrants shall mean the procurement, in order to obtain, directly or indirectly, a financial or other material benefit, of the illegal entry of a person into a State Party of which the person is not a national or a permanent resident. b) 'Illegal entry' shall mean crossing borders without complying with the necessary requirements for legal entry into the receiving State.*"

43 See Gallagher and David (n 33), 555.

44 Massimo Donini, 'Il cittadino extracomunitario da oggetto materiale a tipo d'autore nel controllo penale dell'immigrazione' [2009] Questione giustizia 101 f.; Marco Pelissero 'Il controllo penale del traffico di migranti: il migrante come oggetto e come vittima' in Vincenzo Militello and Alessandro Spena (eds.), *Il traffico di migranti. Diritti, tutele, criminalizzazione* (Giappichelli 2015) 108.

This points to the fact that their position is not that of a victim of smuggling, who would own the protected underlying value impaired by the illicit conduct. The only basis for subjects who entered the territory illegally to request a permanent residence permit on humanitarian grounds is if they were also victims of trafficking, and even so only if they landed in one of the Member States who implemented the invitation to grant such a possibility, set out as purely optional in art. 8 of the UN Protocol.[45]

2.6 The Consequences of the Distinction in European Legal Texts

A corresponding distinction between *"smuggling of migrants"* and *"trafficking in human beings"* also exists at the European level, both in the European Union and in the Council of Europe.

a) The European Union has been dealing with the smuggling phenomenon since 1990,[46] well before the beginning of cooperation in the fields of Justice and Home Affairs, included in the 1992 Maastricht treaty. This interest arose immediately after the fall of the Berlin Wall, with the undermining of traditional borders that had been set after the Second World War.[47] With the dismantling of the opposing political blocs, a significant increase in migration from third countries began.[48] There were two main trajectories of migration: one from East to West and the other from South to North, both converging toward continental Europe.[49]

The reaction of the European Union in the specific criminal field further advanced in 2002, when a directive including definitions and a related

45 However, article 14 sect. 1 of the Protocol recognizes the right of the victims to be recognized as refugees under the 1950 Geneva Convention: see Annoni (n 40), 20 f.

46 According to the Convention implementing the Schengen Agreement of 19 June 1990 (OJ L 239, 22/09/2000), *"the Contracting Parties undertake to impose appropriate penalties on any person who, for financial gain, assists or tries to assist an alien to enter or reside within the territory of one of the Contracting Parties in breach of that Contracting Party's laws on the entry and residence of aliens"* (art. 27.1). On the link between elimination of internal borders and increase in controls at the external borders of the (then) European Community, see Giuseppe Callovi, 'Regulation of immigration in 1993: Pieces of the European Community Jig-Saw Puzzle' [1992] International Migration Review 353 f., 358.

47 Malcom Anderson, 'European Frontiers at the End of the Twentieth Century: an Introduction' in Id. and Eberhardt Bort (eds.), *The frontiers of Europe* (Pinter 1998), 1.

48 See Gallagher and David (n 33), 87. For a critic of the policies against human trafficking Suchland,(n 22), 10 f.

49 Anne Triandafyllidou and Thanos Maroukis, *Migrant Smuggling. Irregular Migration from Asia and Africa to Europe* (Palgrave Macmillan 2012) 1.

Framework Decision were approved.[50] This reflected the positioning of the subject-matter between the first and the third pillar of the European Union, until the "pillar" system was overthrown by the Lisbon Treaty.

The European Union introduced the possibility of imposing binding criminalization standards upon the Member States for the first time precisely in the field of human trafficking. Joint Action 97/154/JHA of 24 February 1997 concerning action to combat trafficking in human beings and sexual exploitation of children was adopted some months before the wide commitment within the "Action plan to combat organized crime",[51] and before the rephrasing of the general provision of the Treaty on the European Union, as amended by the Amsterdam Treaty: it lists trafficking in persons among the criminal areas on which to develop a common action among the Member States (art. 29). The Union would later reaffirm the specific criminal relevance of human trafficking in the Framework Decision 2002/629/JHA of 19 July 2002 and, after the reform of the treaties of Lisbon, in the abovementioned Directive 2011/36/EU of 5 April 2011 on preventing and combating trafficking in human beings and protecting its victims. Here, the role of the issue of human trafficking is once more that of a trailblazer for European intervention in the criminal field: this is the first EU criminal directive approved after the change in the institutional framework due to the Lisbon treaty.[52]

The distinction between the two issues is not airtight: the European Union itself allows some intertwines in the critical Council Directive 2004/81/EC of 29 April 2004, on the residence permit issued to third-country nationals who are victims of trafficking in human beings or who have been the subject of an action to facilitate illegal immigration, who cooperate with competent authorities.[53]

---

50 Art. 1 Council Directive 2002/90/EC of 28 November 2002 defining the facilitation of unauthorised entry, transit and residence; Council Framework Decision 2002/946/JHA of 28 November 2002 on the strengthening of the penal framework to prevent the facilitation of unauthorised entry, transit and residence.

51 Adopted by the Council on 28 April 1997 (97/C 251/01).

52 See the definition of human trafficking in art. 2 of the Directive 2011/36/EU, very similar to that contained in the Protocol to the Palermo Convention (see *infra* nt 65): "*The recruitment, transportation, transfer, harbouring or reception of persons, including the exchange or transfer of control over those persons, by means of the threat or use of force or other forms of coercion, of abduction, of fraud, of deception, of the abuse of power or of a position of vulnerability or of the giving or receiving of payments or benefits to achieve the consent of a person having control over another person, for the purpose of exploitation.*" See *e.g.* Marco Venturoli, 'La direttiva 2011/36/UE: unostrumento completo per contrastare la tratta di esseri umani', in Forlati (ed.) (n 3) 47 f.

53 See Annoni (n 40) 24 f.; Scevi (nt 1), 93 f.

b) With regard to the Council of Europe, its Convention on Action against Trafficking in Human Beings, opened for signature in Warsaw on 16 May 2005, defines the phenomenon with the exact same wording as the relevant above-mentioned UN protocol.[54] Although it purports to adopt a comprehensive and integrated approach to the topic, it does not deal with the other face of migrants' trafficking and therefore reaffirms the strict segregation between the two issues. A common ground can be found in art. 14, which allows the possibility for Member States to implement regulations granting residence permits to trafficking victims, either because of their personal circumstances or because their stay is useful to criminal prosecution of traffickers in the State where they are located.

2.7 The Consequences of the Distinction within the Italian Legal System

From the national perspective too, the distinction between the two kinds of conducts helped clarify at least some of the issues related to migration and allowed for a sharper focus on the different manners in which it presents itself.

The basic distinction in Italy can be summarized merging the features of the two phenomena, as reflected in the internal experience: aiding and abetting illegal immigration ("*favoreggiamento dell'immigrazione clandestina*") refers to "several illegal activities, mainly managed by criminal organizations, also transnational, carrying out the transportation and illegal entry into a foreign state of clandestine migrants, upon their request, and therefore consensually."[55] The spotlight of the criminal offence is on the conduct of transportation and its ability to circumvent border checks on entry into the state's territory. At the same time, the purpose is to profit from the service of transportation of those who entered illegally, so as to acquire, directly or indirectly, a financial or material benefit.

Human trafficking ("*tratta di persone*") encompasses in broad and comprehensive terms all illicit activities aimed at exploiting human beings for criminal

54 The Convention has been ratified in Italy with Law 108 of 2 July 2010, "Ratifica ed esecuzione della Convenzione del Consiglio d'Europa sulla lotta contro la tratta di esseri umani, fatta a Varsavia il 16 maggio 2005, nonché norme di adeguamento dell'ordinamento interno".

55 Filippo Spiezia, 'La tratta di esseri umani: gli strumenti investigativi di cooperazione internazionale', Consiglio Superiore della Magistratura, Roma 14 October 2008, 2 f. (available at www.stranieriinitalia.it/briguglio/immigrazione-e-asilo/2009/agosto/art-spiezia-traff-ess-um.pdf).

purposes after they have been moved to a new context, from the initial offer of illegal services of migrant transportation to recruitment of individuals, sometimes clandestine immigrants. The focus of the relevant illicit conduct is mainly the final exploitation of the migrant.[56]

This distinction between the two illicit conducts is not always properly implemented with regard to their legal relevance and above all to the understanding of the different phenomena. For example, it has been underlined that thanks to this distinction "the moving within the territory of the Union of EU citizens"[57] will not be included in the definition of trafficking. This does not take into account the fact that even in these cases there can be instances of trafficking, as this only depends on the subjugation condition of the victim. Moreover, the distinction is not based on requirements of transnationality or of the involvement of organized criminal groups: these two requirements do not exclusively characterize one of the two illicit conducts. Instead, they are often common to the manner in which both phenomena present themselves, at least in the most serious instances.

In any case, they have their own legal relevance in the Italian legal system as well, following the abovementioned text of the Palermo Convention and its protocols. The most significant impact on the legal system arises out of the criminalisation of each illicit conduct. Smuggling of migrants, narrowly defined, is included in conducts that favour illegal migration: as was previously said, in the First Part of this double issue, it is not regulated by the Penal Code, but by art. 12 TUIMM. Trafficking in human beings is separately criminalised in art. 601 c.p., as a crime against the person and his or her personality.[58]

Art. 12 of the Immigration Law sets forth two different offences. As mentioned above, the basic offence, in sub-sec. 1, focuses on the conduct of transportation of a foreigner into the territory of the state, in violation of the rules and regulation for legal entry detailed in the same law. This represents the typical instance of the crime in question, but it is not exclusive, as the norm also punishes its promotion, direction, organization and financing, as well as all "activities intended to" ease someone's "illegal entry into the territory of the State."[59]

---

56 On this distinction Spiezia (n 54), 3 f.

57 *E.g.* Gabriella Carella, 'La tratta di esseri umani', in Ead. and others, *L'immigrazione e la mobilità delle persone nel diritto dell'Unione Europea* (Monduzzi 2012), 215.

58 Law no. 40 of 6 March 1998 and Law no. 189 of 10 September 2002. See also law no. 228 of 11 August 2003 for the reform of arts. 600, 601 and 602 c.p., and d.lgs. no. 24 of 4 March 2014, implementing Directive 2011/36/EC.

59 See Pelissero (n 44), 110.

The second criminal conduct, set forth in sub-sec. 3, is a "special" and more serious one: in this case the conduct criminalized in the first paragraph takes place in a specific context, with aggravating features, more dangerous because of the number of trafficked persons (five or more: letter a), of the number of traffickers (three or more), of the form of transport (letter d), or the available resources (lett. e). The specific point of view of migrants' protection is relevant with regard to dangers linked to the basic conduct of aiding and abetting illegal immigration (letters b and c).

Before each of these two provisions there is a clause establishing that, if a conduct is also punishable according to a norm with higher criminal sanctions toward the *actus reus* they cover, only the most severe provision will apply: this is a so-called clause of absorption or consumption ("*assorbimento o consunzione*") or safeguard clause ("*clausola di riserva*"), stating that the norm will apply "unless the action constitutes a more serious criminal offence" ("*salvo che il fatto non costituisca più grave reato*"). The relationship between this clause and other offences that may be relevant to assess the legal classifications of the facts linked to the condition of migrants, specifically the crime of human trafficking and how it has been interpreted in Italian case law, will be investigated below.

Preliminarily, the legal relevance of trafficking in human beings, criminalized in Italy by art. 601 of the Penal Code, will be analysed.

The current wording is the result of many subsequent normative interventions, which have progressively implemented international texts on this issue. The basis for these interventions was the original text of art. 601 of the Penal Code of 1930. There, trafficking in slaves, not in persons, was punished, even though the legal condition of slavery had long been abolished by then. Trafficking in persons "in conditions analogous to slavery" was recognised as equivalent to trafficking in slaves. This phrasing is the same as adopted by art. 600, already present as Art. 145 of the Penal Code of 1889: it punished "enslavement" and it referred to slavery as a legal status where a human being loses entitlement to any right and becomes the subject of someone else's property rights. The conditions analogous to slavery were also narrowly construed, to avoid excessive vagueness, so as to mean other similar and legally relevant forms of subjugation. Instead, the *de facto* conditions of subjugation of a person to another were not encompassed by either the norms on enslavement of the 1930 code or those of the older one.

The norm on enslavement, as it was written, lacked any real scope of application. For that reason, before the 1930 code was approved, there had been a debate on the need to criminalise trafficking and trade in slaves, to prevent and combat the introduction into Italian territory of persons coming from other legal systems where slavery had not been abolished yet.[60]

On that ground, in the 1930 code trafficking was a separate criminal offence, maintaining the double terms "slavery and conditions analogous thereto", always referring to legally relevant relationships. *De facto* slavery situations were relevant under the new offence of coercion ("*plagio*"), aimed at combating situations where a subject was put in a condition of total submission to another.

Thus, the scope of application of trafficking was substantially reduced, and as a crime it remained essentially unenforced for a long period, also because it was hard to prove all elements of the offence. Even then, relevant sources of international law—*i.e.* the 1926 Geneva Convention (ratified by Royal Decree n. 1723 of 26 April 1928) and the supplementary convention of 7 September 1956 (ratified by Law n. 1304 of 20 December 1957)—included within the conditions analogous to that of a slave the conditions of merely factual relationships and contexts, *e.g.* the woman who cannot refuse to marry a man who pays a sum of money to obtain her.[61]

The real trigger to changing the relationship between the norms in question was the judgment of the Italian Constitutional Court (no. 96 of 1981) which declared the crime of *plagio* unconstitutional for excessive vagueness.[62] Without that norm, the instances of *de facto* subjugation would be left unpunished. The debate on the notion of "conditions analogous to slavery" pursuant to arts. 600 and 601 c.p. was therefore rekindled, as it was the only appropriate way to bridge the newly-formed gap through interpretation.[63] Indeed, the interpretation mentioned disclosed risks of vagueness in that wording too: the explicit reference to analogy was not backed by the conditions that normally allow for said interpretative method in the field of criminal law, as a previous listing of

60 See Scevi (n 14), 33 f.; Giovanni Caruso, *Delitti di schavitù e dignità umana nella riforma degli art. 600, 601, 602 del c.p.* (Cedam 2005) 63.

61 *E.g.* Francesco Salerno, 'Evoluzione e determinatezza del divieto di tratta nel diritto penale internazionale ed italiano', in *Studi di diritto internazionale in onore di Arangio-Ruiz* (Editoriale Scientifica 2004) 2116.

62 Constitutional Court 8 June 1981 no. 96, in *Rivista italiana diritto e procedura penale* 1981, 1147 f. with comment by Marco Boscarelli; in *Giurisprudenza Costituzionale* 1981, 806 with comment by P.G. Grasso.

63 See in case law the judgments of the Italian Supreme Court of Cassation: Cass., Sec. III, 19 Februar 2004, in *Cass. penale*, 2005, 786; Cass., Sec. III, 19 Mai 1998 in *Diritto penale e processo*, 1998, 1085; Cass., Sec. V, 19 December 1997, in *Giustizia Penale* 1998, II, 399; Cass., United sections, 20 November 1996, in *Cassazione penale* 1997, 1308. On the topic see also Scevi (n 14) 41 f.; Caruso (n 60) 66 f.; Bartolomeo Romano, 'Riflessioni penalistiche sulle misure contro la tratta di persone' [2006] L'indice penale 661 [and also Id., *Reati contro la persona. III. Reati contro la libertà individuale* (Giuffrè 2016), 24 f.].

terms in the same norms that may circumscribe its meaning. The notion of "servitude" does not have rigid boundaries beyond the examples set forth in international conventions. It is therefore not useful to define the scope of the factual situations that may be covered by it.[64]

In the end, the wording of the crime of trafficking in art. 601 c.p., as well as that of enslavement in art. 600 c.p., was overcome not by the issues of non-compliance with the principles of precision and definiteness of the conducts described; it was the increasingly multi-layered framework of criminal law, of which the field in question is a prime example. As highlighted above, the rise of migrations and of international mobility of persons elicited the attention of international law on trafficking. Changes in the Italian legal system mirrored the evolution of international sources in this field.

Specifically, the definition of trafficking in art. 601 was amended a first time by law no. 228 of 11 August 2003: it introduced actions against human trafficking to ensure the compliance of Italy with the already recalled Framework Decision 2002/629/JHA of 19 July 2002. A decade later, supranational inputs were reflected in a new definition of trafficking, adjusted through legislative decree 24 of 4 March 2014 to implement Directive 2011/36/EU of 5 April 2011, previously mentioned, on preventing and combating trafficking in human beings and protecting its victims.

The result is the current wording of the offence of trafficking in art. 601 c.p., which still maintains the distinctive traits of its mainspring, the UN Protocol on Trafficking in Human Beings, which influenced all subsequent international sources in the field:

> Whoever recruits, introduces into the territory of the State, transfers even outside said territory, transports, yields authority over a person to another person, offers lodging to one or more persons who are in the conditions specified in article 600; or performs the said conducts against one or more persons by deceit, violence, threats, abuse of power or taking advantage of a situation of vulnerability or of a condition of physical or psychic inferiority or of need, or by promising or giving money or any other advantage to the person having control over that person, for the purpose of inducing or forcing them to perform work, sexual services or begging or, in any case, to perform unlawful activities entailing their exploitation or removal of organs, shall be punished with imprisonment from eight to twenty years.[65]

64 See Salerno (n 61) 2119.

65 For the definition of art. 2 of the Directive 2011/36/EU see n 52.

> The aforesaid penalty shall apply also to whoever performs the said conducts, even without using the above means, against a minor.

A separate and different normative consideration of smuggling and trafficking emerges from the Italian legal system, prompted by the parallel distinction present since the UN Convention and its protocols. Nevertheless, this cannot conceal the fact that in practice they are not two fully different phenomena, being more of two different manifestations of the same phenomenon, often so intertwined that they become indistinguishable.[66]

As already noted elsewhere, there are several features of international mobility of persons where abstract clarity of boundaries between the two kinds of events fades. Frequently, a migrant begins his journey within a smuggling operation but once he reaches a foreign country he becomes a victim of forms of personal exploitation that can escalate up to slavery. There is a high risk of being entrapped in deceits, wrongdoings and blackmails, directed at exploitation, for those who pursue better living conditions than in their home country and to that end turn to groups and subjects who act illegally to take them across the physical and legal boundaries between states. The cases of men and women who are forced into illegal labour or prostitution once they have reached their destination to pay off the price of the journey are paradigmatic.[67]

Besides, it should be at least questioned whether the social and personal circumstances that migrants try to escape are irrelevant to the willingness of the decision to leave, as in most cases they exert such great pressure and urgency that an assessment of the action as a free choice is flawed. In the actual interaction between relevant subjects, the migrants' condition of particular weakness, even merely economical, makes their relationship with the organization which transports them to another country resemble the situation of exploitation typical of human trafficking. Notwithstanding the abstract distinction prevailing in the legal perspective, it is increasingly clear that smuggled migrants can be victims of an offence to their human dignity, albeit often in merely prodromal forms, different than those typical of the offence of trafficking.

---

66 Spiezia (n 54) 4; Nicoletta Parisi, 'I limiti posti dal diritto internazionale alle scelte di penalizzazionedel legislatore internoin materia di immigrazione irregolare', in Rosaria Sicurella (ed.), *Il controllo penale dell'immigrazione irregolare: esigenze di tutela, tentazioni simboliche, imperativi garantistici* (Giappichelli 2012) 89; Pelissero (n 44), 105.

67 Vincenzo Militello and Alessandro Spena, *"La cruna dell'ago": il migrante fra mobilità e controllo*, Introduction to Id./Id. (eds.) (n 44) 4 f., 8 f. See also Bernasconi (n 3) 87 f.

2.8 The Consequences for Internal Case Law: Multiplicity of Offences or (Apparent) Conflict of Norms?

Returning to the legal classification of the two conducts after reflecting upon the actual structure of the issues, the most interesting element appears to be the relationship between the two criminal offences as interpreted in Italian case law.

Faced with the normative frameworks described, Italian judges have only partially taken into account the substantial links existing between the two phenomena, and this has provoked uncertainty regarding the relationship between the two offences.

On the one side, the facts underlying trafficking and smuggling have been correctly identified as potentially placed on a continuum of activities in reality: in smuggling cases there should be the consent of the foreign subject, but the presence of an initial consent can be tainted by deceit if the aim of the trafficker is to enslave people once they reach their destination.[68]

On the other side, the offence of aiding and abetting illegal immigration has not always been held to be subsidiary to the more serious offence of trafficking pursuant to art. 601, and therefore not applied because of the principle of absorption of a less serious offence into a more serious one.

The latter point is particularly meaningful for the legal relevance of the relationship between the two phenomena: a first standpoint applied the principle of absorption, at least in cases where assisting illegal entry of a foreigner into a state's territory was aimed at carrying out human trafficking, since the first conduct would merely be a portion of a bigger scheme that can only be properly classified as a whole as trafficking.[69]

The Supreme Court of Cassation has recently shifted its approach and supported a very strict theory, with a decision grounded on the following rationale. The specific judgment sets the boundaries between the two offences relying on a narrow construction of the safeguard clause, limiting its application only to cases where "the more serious offence protects the same legal interest."[70] Based on this, the reasoning recalls the traditional belief that the underlying legal interest in the offence of aiding and abetting illegal immigration is the state's interest in controlling migration flows, even in the cases of those aggravating circumstances, mentioned above, where it is undeniable that weak subjects who are victims of trafficking migrants are explicitly considered.

68 See Cass., Sec. V, 24 September 2010, no. 40045.

69 See Cass., Sec. V, 25 March 2010, no. 20740.

70 See Cass., Sec. III, 8 October 2015, no. 5056.

According to the Court, a totally different interpretation, construing "the safety of the migrant" as a "specific and direct object of criminal protection" would have entailed the aggravating circumstances giving rise to a separate offence, which the Court would have preferred but is not allowed by the text of the article. They then proceed to compare it to the offence of trafficking in human beings, where the legal interest protected is the human personality, and they refuse to recognize any absorption of the former offence into the latter: the legal interests protected seem overly diverse. The Court even denies that the offence of aiding and abetting illegal immigration may be "pluri-offensive", that is protecting more than one legal interest. They thus exclude the relationship between the two norms including even a partial contact that would be reconciled with the absorption, within the offence of trafficking, of the other offence as its harbinger. It should be more carefully assessed whether there is at least partial co-existence of protected legal interests between the two offences; regardless of this, the faulty point in the Court's reasoning can be traced back to the willingness to look for a relationship of abstract speciality between the two norms, which is not present.

Indeed, it is only when one norm is more specific, or special, than the other that the identity of the action must be questioned in logical terms: it would not be possible to erase the special norm without leaving the action unpunished, because it would not be included within the more general norm. But the safeguard clause present in the article on aiding and abetting illegal immigration is not one of speciality but of consumption: in these cases, the term "same fact" should not be read in merely logical terms but it should be confronted with the actual ways in which the facts present themselves in reality.

In the end, if it all comes back to the phenomena sharing traits in reality, as explained above, the common framework where the substantial issue lies is striking. In this perspective, it is apparent that the diversity in the protected legal interests cannot be the sole prerequisite for the application of the specific safeguard clause; otherwise, it would be deprived of any practical significance.

Besides, a comparison with other norms reveals precisely that the diversity of protected legal interest is not a relevant element in the rational interpretation of the safeguard clause in the offence of aiding and abetting illegal immigration. Indeed, with regard to the relationship between the same norm and a different offence, this diversity of protected legal interests did not previously mean that the application of the absorption principle was prevented. The same subdivision ("*Sezione*") of the Supreme Court of Cassation had in the past correctly applied the absorption of the conduct of aiding and abetting illegal immigration into the more serious offence of fostering prostitution, provided that the actual facts at issue coincided.[71]

The attempt to stress the differences between the conduct of migrant smuggling and human trafficking so that both offences can be charged neglects some links in the legal relevance of the two phenomena. An example is the inclusion of the situations of need ("*necessità*") among the conducts punished by art. 600 c.p. as a "state of continuative subjugation" ("*stato di soggezione continuativa*").

Case law has interpreted the term "situation of need" as "any situation of weakness or material or moral lack that can influence the will of a person"; it is not the legal defence known as necessity *ex* art. 54 c.p.[72] In fact, the same case law states that it coincides with the definition of "position of vulnerability" set forth in art. 1, sub-sec. 1, letter c of the Framework Council Decision 2002/629/JHA and then recalled in art. 2, sub-sec. 2 of the 2011 EU Directive on Human Trafficking.[73] There, it is described as "a situation in which the person concerned has no real or acceptable alternative but to submit to the abuse involved": this definition, though, recalls the impossibility to act otherwise, which is no less intense than that relevant as a criminal defence pursuant to art. 54.

To overcome this contradiction in the reference texts for the definition of human trafficking, it should be agreed that the degree of influence exerted over a persons' decisions should not exclude every possibility to act otherwise: it should already be relevant in cases where the conduct is one of exploitation of an individual weakness that has an impact on the capability of self-determination of the subject. This relative influence should be acknowledged in many of the situations where migrants turn to a trafficker so that they can be transported to another country, at least in cases where their request is rooted in a situation of economic need that pushes them to try to improve their condition and that of their closest relatives. This feature is therefore a liaison between the two conducts of illegal migration and trafficking in human beings. It shows that, even when the respective conducts are not exactly identical from a naturalistic perspective, they can be considered as identical from a legal perspective, at least in some instances. Thus the abovementioned safeguard clause would be provided with limited scope of application: at least in cases where in reality the situations of exploitation of the victims' vulnerability is

71 Cass., Sec. III, 2 October 2013, no. 46223.

72 Cass., Sec. V, 6 Mai 2010 no. 21630.

73 Cass., Sec. III, 12 March 2009 no. 13734.

identical, the more serious offence (i.e. human trafficking) will prevail and the less serious one (aiding and abetting illegal immigration) will be absorbed and not applied.

2.9 Short Conclusion

Human trafficking is a type of criminal offence which spread in parallel to the phenomena of globalization and increase in human mobility. The strategies to combat it are made challenging by the fact that it often remains "undercover." Only a comprehensive perspective on the various forms in which it can exist and on their relevant causes can aspire to be successful.

The distinction between migrant smuggling and human trafficking, deeply rooted in international, European and national legislation, is nowadays being interpreted by Italian case law in a rigid way with closed walls.

The ongoing issue should instead be considered focusing, first and foremost, on the protection of human dignity. This may foster a better understanding of the osmotic feature of the borderline between the two illicit activities, without denying theoretical differences, but at the same time without neglecting their actual and frequent intertwinings.

Bibliography

Albrecht, Hans-Jörg and Cyrille Fijnaut (eds.), *The Containment of Transnational Organized Crime. Comments of the UN Convention of December 2000*, (Iuscrim 2002).

Anderson, Malcom, 'European Frontiers at the End of the Twentieth Century: an Introduction' in Id. and Eberhardt Bort (eds.), *The frontiers of Europe* (Pinter 1998) 1.

Annoni, Alessandra, 'Gli obblighi internazionali in materia di tratta degli esseri umani', in Serena Forlati (ed.), *La lotta alla tratta di esseri umani fra dimensione internazionale e ordinamento interno* (Jovene 2013) 1.

Aradau, Claudia, 'The Perverse Politics of Four-Letter Word: Risk and Pity in the Securitisation of Human Trafficking' [2004] *Millenium: Journal of international Studies* 251.

Bales, Kevin, *Disposable people. New Slavery in the Global Economy* (1999) it. ed. *I nuovi schiavi. La merce umana nell'economia globale* (Feltrinelli 2004).

Barbieri, Maria Cristina, 'La riduzione in schiavitù: un passato che non vuole passare. Un'indagine storica sulla costruzione e i limiti del tipo' [2010] Materiali per una storia della cultura giuridica, 229.

Bernasconi, Costanza, 'La repressione penale della tratta di esseri umani nell'ordinamento italiano, in Serena Forlati (ed.), *La lotta alla tratta di esseri umani fra dimensione internazionale e ordinamento interno* (Jovene 2013) 69.

Boister, Neil, *An Introduction to Transnational Criminal Law* (Oxford University Press 2011).

Bruckmüller, Karin and Stepan Schumann, 'Crime control versus Social Work Approaches in the Context of the "3P" Paradigm' in John Winterdyk, Benjamin Perrin and Philip Reichel (eds.), *Human trafficking. Exploring the International Nature, Concerns and Complexities* (CRC Press 2012) 103.

Brysk, Alison and Austin Choi-Fitzpatrick, 'Rethinking Trafficking', in Id. and Id. (eds.), *From Human Trafficking to Human Rights: Reframing Contemporary Slavery* (University of Pennsylvania 2012) 1.

Callovi, Giuseppe, 'Regulation of immigration in 1993: Pieces of the European Community Jig-Saw Puzzle' [1992] International Migration Review 353.

Carella, Gabriella, 'La tratta di esseri umani', in Ead. and others, *L'immigrazione e la mobilità delle persone nel diritto dell'Unione Europea* (Monduzzi 2012), 207.

Centonze, Alessandro, *Criminalità organizzata e reati transnazionali* (Giuffrè 2008)

Chuang, Janie, 'Beyond a Snapshot: Preventing Human Trafficking in the Global Economy' [2006] Indiana Journal of Global Legal Studies 136.

Communication from the Commission to the EU-Parlament and other of 19 June 2012 COM(2012) 286 fin, 'EU Strategy towards the Eradication of Trafficking in Human Beings 2012–2016'.

Ćopić, Sanja and Biljana Simeunović-Patić, 'Victims of Human Trafficking. Meeting Victim/s Needs?', in John Winterdyk, Benjamin Perrin and Philip Reichel (eds.), *Human trafficking. Exploring the International Nature, Concerns and Complexities* (CRC Press 2012) 265.

Decker, Scott, 'Human Trafficking: context and connections to conventional crime' [2015] *Journal of Crime and Justice* 291.

Di Martino, Alberto, 'Criminalità organizzata e reato transnazionale, diritto penale nazionale: l'attuazione in Italia della c.d. Convenzione di Palermo' [2007] Diritto penale e processo 15.

Donini, Massimo, 'Il cittadino extracomunitario da oggetto materiale a tipo d'autore nel controllo penale dell'immigrazione' [2009] Questione giustizia 101.

Faraldo Cabana, Patricia, *Asociaciones ilícitas y organizaciones criminales en el código penal español* (Tirant lo Blanc 2012).

Gallagher, Anne, *The International Law of Human Trafficking* (Cambridge University Press 2010).

Gallagher, Anne and Fiona David, *The International Law of Migrant Smuggling* (Cambridge University Press 2010).

Global Report on Trafficking in Persons 2016 (UNODC 2017) available at https://www.unodc.org/documents/data-and-analysis/glotip/2016_Global_Report_on_Trafficking_in_Persons.pdf.

Hathaway, James 'The Human Rights Quagmire of "Human Trafficking"' [2008] Virginia Journal of International Law 30.

Hepburn, Stephanie and Luise Simon, *Human Trafficking Around the World* (Columbia University Press 2013).

Janssens, Stef, 'Fenomeenanalyse van mensenhandel' in Charles-Éric Clesse (ed.) *Traite des être humains Mensenhandel—Mensenmokkel* (Die Keure, 2010) 39.

Jonsson, Anna, 'Introduction', in Ead. (ed.), *Human Trafficking and Human Security* (Routeledge 2009) 1.

Kneebone, Susan and Julie Debeljak, *Transnational crime and Human Rights. Responses to Human Trafficking in the Greater Mekong Region* (Routledge 2012).

Krieg, Sarah, 'Trafficking in human beings: The EU approach between border control, law enforcement and human rights' [2009] European Law Journal 775.

Lee, Maggy, *Trafficking and Global Crime Control* (Sage 2011).

Leman, Johan and Stef Janssens, *Human Trafficking and Migrant Smuggling in Southeast Europe and Russia. Learning Criminal Entrepreneurship and Traditional Culture* (Palgrave Macmillan 2015).

Lindner, Christoph, *Die Effektivität transnationaler Maßnahmen gegen Menschenhandel in Europa* (Mohr Siebeck 2014).

Maljević, Almir, *'Participation in a Criminal Organisation' and 'Conspiracy'* (Duncker & Humblot 2011).

Mancini, David, 'Il cammino europeo nel contrasto alla tratta di persone' [2010] Diritto Penale e Processo 7.

McClean, John D., *Transnational Organized Crime. A commentary on the UN Convention and its Protocols* (Oxford University Press 2007).

Michelini, Gualtiero and Gioacchino Polimeni, 'Il fenomeno del crimine transnazionale e la convenzione delle NU contro il crimine organizzato transnazionale', in Elisabetta Rosi (ed.), *Criminalità organizzata transnazionale e sistema penale italiano* (IPSOA 2007) 1.

Militello, Vincenzo, 'Le strategie di contrasto della criminalità organizzata transnazionale tra esigenze di politica criminale e tutela dei diritti umani', in Carola Parano and Alessandro Centonze (eds.), *L'attività di contrasto alla criminalità organizzata. Lo stato dell'arte* (Giuffrè 2005) 243.

Militello, Vincenzo and Alessandro Spena, *"La cruna dell'ago": il migrante fra mobilità e controllo*, Introduction to Id. and Id. (eds.) *Il traffico di migranti. Diritti, tutele, criminalizzazione* (Giappichelli 2015) 1.

Mishra, Veerendra, 'Introduction', in Id. (ed.), *Human Trafficking. The stakeholders' perspective* (Sage 2013) 1.

Nilken, David, 'Human Trafficking and Legal Culture' [2010] Israel law review 481.

Obokata, Tom, *Trafficking in Human Beings from a Human Rights Perspective: Towards a more Holistic Approach* (Martinus Nijhoff Publishers 2006).

Pandey, Arumendra K., 'Economic Rehabilitation: A human approach to combat human trafficking', in Veerendra Mishra (ed.), *Human Trafficking. The stakeholders' perspective* (Sage 2013) 340.

Parisi, Francesco, 'Il contrasto al traffico di esseri umani fra modelli normativi e risultati applicativi' [2016] Rivista italiana di diritto e procedura penale 1763.

Parisi, Nicoletta, 'I limiti posti dal diritto internazionale alle scelte di penalizzazionedel legislatore internoin materia di immigrazione irregolare', in Rosaria Sicurella (ed.), *Il controllo penale dell'immigrazione irregolare: esigenze di tutela, tentazioni simboliche, imperativi garantistici* (Giappichelli 2012) 89.

Pelissero, Marco 'Il controllo penale del traffico di migranti: il migrante come oggetto e come vittima', in Vincenzo Militello and Alessandro Spena (eds.), *Il traffico di migranti. Diritti, tutele, criminalizzazione* (Giappichelli 2015) 105.

Planitzer, Julia, *Trafficking in Human Beings and Human Rights* (Neuer Wissenschaftlicher Verlag 2014).

Ponti, Gianluca, *Crimini transnazionali e diritto internazionale* (Giuffrè 2010).

Report of the Experts Group on Trafficking in Human Beings (Brussels 2004) available at http://www.institut-fuer-menschenrechte.de/fileadmin/user_upload/PDF-Dateien/EU-Dokumente/report_of_the_experts_group_on_trafficking_in_human_beings_2004.pdf.

Rijken, Connie, 'A Human Rights Based Approach to Trafficking in Human Beings' [2009] Security and Human Rights 212.

Salt, John and Jeremy Stein, 'Migration as a Business: the case of Trafficking' [1997] Intern. Migration 467.

Scarpa, Silvia, *Trafficking in Human Beings. Modern Slavery* (Oxford University Press 2008).

Scevi, Paola, *Nuove schiavitù e diritto penale* (Giuffrè 2014).

Segrave, Marie, *Human Trafficking* (Ashgate 2013).

Shelley, Louise, 'Human Security and Human Trafficking', in Anna Jonsson (ed.), *Human Trafficking and Human Security* (Routeledge 2009) 10.

Shelley, Louise, *Human Trafficking. A Global Perspective* (Cambridge University Press 2010).

Spiezia, Filippo, 'La tratta di esseri umani: gli strumenti investigativi di cooperazione internazionale', Consiglio Superiore della Magistratura, Roma 14 October 2008, 2 f. (available at www.stranieriinitalia.it/briguglio/immigrazione-e-asilo/2009/agosto/art-spiezia-traff-ess-um.pdf).

Stoecker, Sally and Louise Shelley (eds.), *Human Trafficking and Transnational Crime: Eurasian and American perspectives* (Rowman & Littlefield 2005).

Suchland, Jennifer, *Economies of violence. Transnational feminism, Postsocialism and the Politics of Sex Trafficking* (Duke University Press 2015).

Tschorr, Sophie, *Trafficking of human beings* (Oldenburger Verlag für Wirtschaft, Informatik und Recht 2015).

Turner, Jackie and Liz Kelly, 'Trade Secrets: Intersections between Diasporas and Crime Groups in the Constitution of the Human Trafficking Chain' [2009] British Journal of Criminology 184.

Vlassis, Dimitri, 'The UN Convention against Transnational Organized Crime', in Mats Berdal and Monica Serrano (eds.), *Transnational Organized Crime and International Security: Business as Usual* (Lyenne Renner 2002) 83.

Wörner, Liane, 'Penal theory and the protection of life—the human dignity argument and its inconsistencies in German criminal law', in Arndt Sinn (ed.), *Menschenrechte und Strafrecht*, (V&R unipress 2013) 25.

Yea, Sallie (ed.), *Human Trafficking in Asia. Forcing issues* (Routledge 2015).

Zibas, Karolis, 'Exploitative Sham Marriages and Trafficking in Human Beings in Lithuania', in Minna Viuhko and others (eds.), *Exploitative Sham Marriages: Exploring the Links between Human Trafficking and Sham Marriages in Estonia, Ireland, Latvia, Lithuania and Slovakia* (HEUNI 2016) 254 (available at http://www.heuni.fi/material/attachments/heuni/reports/ci5Y5cgbB/Nettiin.pdf).

Zúñiga Rodriguez, Laura, *Criminalidad organizada y sistema de derecho penal* (Comares 2009).

www.ingramcontent.com/pod-product-compliance
Lightning Source LLC
Chambersburg PA
CBHW031332230926
51848CB00001B/201

* 9 7 8 9 0 0 4 4 0 1 6 6 2 *